Kingdom Connection

Where Wonder Awaits

Discovering the Presence, Power, and Plan of God

J. A. McPhail

Rowe Publishing

ISBN 13: 978-1-64446-012-2

Cover photo by Mark Iwig Photography. Used by permission.
markiwigphotography.smugmug.com

Scripture taken from:

The Message by Eugene Peterson. Copyright 1993, 1994, 1995, 1996, 2000, 2001, 2002. Used by permission of NavPress Publishing Group.

Contemporary English Version. Copyright © 1995 by American Bible Society.

New King James Version. Copyright © 1982 by Thomas Nelson. Used by permission. All rights reserved.

King James Version. Public Domain.

NCV The Holy Bible, New Century Version®. Copyright © 2005 by Thomas Nelson, Inc.

1 3 5 7 9 8 6 4 2

Printed in the United States of America
Published by

Rowe Publishing
www.rowepub.com

Praise for
Kingdom Corner Connection

Kingdom Corner Connection takes the truth of God's word, and the fullness of the Kingdom available to every believer, and gives practical advice on how to walk it out. Within the pages of this book is the testimony of a faithful God that gives each reader permission to believe for their own Kingdom breakthrough. J.A. McPhail takes phrases such as "Kingdom living" and "the plan of God" and explains them into every day concepts through her own life experiences with relevant scripture woven in between.

Each person's relationship with the Lord is the most important relationship we will ever tend to. Good communication with the Lord through reading His word, prayer and intercession is critical to fostering that relationship. *Kingdom Corner Connection* is an excellent tool to help us engage in more communication for a better relationship with our Creator and King.

Melissa Joy Wright
Evangelist and Prayer Pastor for
Becoming Love Ministries Association
www.BecomingLoveMinistries.com

From the author of the well-known *Tresia* series comes this refreshing autobiographical-style work on living life with a Kingdom of God outlook.

Each brief chapter is filled with poignant insights and Scripture passages which remind us of our longing for connection and home. If you're a fan of music, reading, creativity, and family … you'll love *Kingdom Corner Connection* by my friend J.A. McPhail. This book will end up on your bedside table!

Dr. Paul Pettit, speaker, and
Author of *Christ-Centered Masculinity*
President & Founder, Dynamic Dads
www.dynamicdads.com

If you want to know what *Kingdom Corner Connection* is all about, here it is in author J.A. McPhail's own words. "...encouraging you to spend enough time with God to know Him and to live well in His Kingdom."

Deftly and creatively woven with her own life experiences, *Kingdom Corner Connection* is written from a place of humility and vulnerability, and imparts fresh and creative ideas of how each of us can spend quality, make-a-difference-time with God—the God Who "knows exactly where I am and how I got here."

A must-have guide for all devoted Kingdom-dwellers.

Deb Gorman / Debo Publishing
Author of *Who Are These People:*
Spiritual Lessons In Obscurity, Books One
and Two and *Leaving Your Lover*
www.debggorman.com

Kingdom Corner Connection: *Where Wonder Awaits*; those words are music to my ears! I have been a pastor's wife for over ten years and I would love to see all born again believers grasp the concepts hidden within these pages. Our daily walk is all about relationship with the Father. He longs to know us and for us to know Him. J.A. McPhail has done a phenomenal job explaining the tools we have been given to be successful in connecting and building the Kingdom of God.

I personally had a deep connection with *Part II: The Corner*. My personal experiences in my Kingdom Corner are sometimes beyond words. That is an essential place for every child of God. If you don't have a Kingdom Corner you have no idea what you are missing out on! There is nothing like the comfort, peace, encouragement, and guidance from the "Cornerman." Open your hearts and get ready to be challenged and charged for your Kingdom assignment.

Sarah C. Cooke, Pastor's wife,
West Asheboro Church of God, Asheboro, NC
www.westasheborocog.org

Hebrews 11:1 tells us that faith is *"the assurance of things hoped for, the conviction of things not seen."* In the 50 years that I have known this author, I can testify that her life has been a constant demonstration of a life of faith in her Lord. This book chronicles many key events from her life's faith journey, with all of its ups and downs. It will also serve as a challenge to those who read it to fol-low a similar path of faith. I personally owe Jeannie a huge debt of gratitude for how she reached out to share her faith with me, when our friendship began when we were in high school together.

Bob Iwig, (The Bob in Chapter 10!)
Associate Pastor, Hope Bible Fellowship,
Noblesville, IN
www.hopebiblefellowship.net

Dear reader, please be sure to take the time to read this beautiful book. It is my favorite book by J.A. McPhail. The author grabbed me from the beginning to the end. I loved how she wove per-sonal testimony and spiritual truth together into its pages. From relating about going through a tornado, noting the parallel of the the Unshakable Kingdom, J.A. keeps you enchanted and inspired. She, like Jesus, is a true storyteller, and you will be blessed from start to finish. Every page will keep your attention, from song titles to Raggedy Ann, to her daughter's Coca-Cola collection to personal directives. Prepare to be challenged, blessed and inspired.

Dr. Barri Cae Seif, Author of
The Name, Hashem, speaker, and
Founder of Sar Shalom Israel, Ovilla, TX
www.sarshalomisrael.org

Foreword

Most of us enter into relationships with the wind at our backs, joy in our hearts, and desires for the future. Marriage, dating, friendship, family, no matter the relationship, we all learn that trust and communication must be established for it to be healthy. When it comes to our relationship with the Almighty God, these are not only healthy but essential.

In *Kingdom Corner Connection*, J.A. McPhail paints a beautifully honest picture of the dedication a relationship with Jesus requires. Her vulnerability to share her own life experiences as examples woven and spun with the truth of Scripture is refreshing and encouraging. In our current society and state, her picture of how we choose to live out our trust in God and communicate with Him through the power of prayer presents a true form reality to what our Creator can do when we seek first His Kingdom each and every day.

We are called as children of the King to put on His armor each day, accepting the position to which He calls, in order that we may conquer the battlefield of this life. McPhail encourages this in the book stating, *"All you have to do is enter your Kingdom Corner and call on Him."*

Many books have influenced my heart and my ministry, and *Kingdom Corner Connection* is not an exception. I believe your heart will be truly touched and encouraged by an author who is not just writing but living the words in this book. I may have a greater insight into that since I have the privilege of calling the author Aunt JA!

If you are seeking a book to help you feel good about quiet time, then this is not the book for you. However, if you are seeking a book to challenge the very essence of what it means to communicate and live in the presence of God – then dive in with your whole heart! Truly, we all need to, *"Experience the Kingdom Corner Connection...where wonder awaits."*

Luke Aadalen
Lead Pastor, Kingfisher Federated Church
Singer\Songwriter
YouTube: 2 Mile Pastor

Dedicated to the pastors, preachers, and teachers who shared the Bible with me and continue to preach and teach the uncompromised Word of God to the world.

———◆———

And to my husband Dennis, who encouraged me to write this book because he knows how making Kingdom Corner time a priority every day has made all the difference in our life and ministry.

Contents

PART I

THE KINGDOM

King'dom, *noun*

The territory or country subject to a king; an undivided territory under the dominion of a king or monarch.

In Scripture, the government or universal dominion of God.

————————◆————————

Jesus asked, "Are you starting to get a handle on all this?"

They answered, "Yes."

*He said, "Then you see how every student well-trained in God's **Kingdom** is like the owner of a general store who can put his hands on anything you need, old or new, exactly when you need it."*

Matthew 13:51-52 The Message (MSG)

Chapter One

Kingdom Living

Vehicles lined both sides of the road, attesting to the size of the crowd gathered inside the grand restored building. The twang of bluegrass instruments drifted through the rusty screen door, serenading visitors as we drew near the worn stone steps of the front entrance. Stepping inside was like taking a time machine back to the late 1800's. The musty smell of old wood and antiques rose from the shelves that lined both walls of the large room and mingled with the delicious aroma of fresh-brewed coffee and pastries. I was thrilled to find this place!

Old General Stores are fascinating to me. I enjoy visiting them and hearing how everything a customer could have wanted was stacked on the shelves, ready and available, or could be ordered even if a special delivery was necessary. A General Store was also a place where neighbors came for activities, conversation, and fellowship. It was a gathering place that filled the needs of its patrons, as well as many of their heart's desires.

When Dennis and I first moved to Cowee Valley in Western North Carolina, one of the first places we visited was the old Rickman General Store, strategically located on the bend in the road that led to our property. After a few visits, we discovered that the land we bought used to be owned by Mr. Rickman, and we had acquired it from his daughter.

Several years earlier, local residents of the valley decided to band together to save and restore this historical neighborhood store. Today, from May through December, guest musicians and storytellers come from all over the area to share with visitors their gifts of music and stories. The sounds of banjos, guitars, dulcimers, singing, and conversation fill the daytime hours every Saturday of the season. Volunteers are on site to provide refreshments, tales, and share information about artifacts from our valley's past history and present activities.

As a new member of the community, I had the privilege of sharing my books on the last day of the 2019 season. The combination of music and presenting my books created about the most fun I've had since becoming an author! Plus, they've graciously allowed me to stock my books for sale. That same day I also met a man named Larry who bought our testimony book, *I Will Not Fear: A Chosen Life.* A couple weeks later, he texted me after he'd read it and asked if he could send me a Bible verse by text every morning. Doing this for a list of people was his ministry. I accepted and God has used that verse every day to speak to me. Larry has prayed for me as I have been writing this book and he has been such an encourager to me as an author. A chance meeting at the local general store brought me the blessing of a new friend, prayer partner, and a dose of the Word of God every day. That's how God connects us to exactly what we need.

I think that's why the Message translation of Matthew 13: 51-52 resonated with me on such a deep level. This analogy of Kingdom living is so easy to understand. If it is promised in the Bible, whatever we need or desire as children of God and citizens of the Kingdom, is ready and available for the asking, already in stock! Even if we pray for something and the need for right timing causes the delivery to be delayed, we can rest assured that whatever it is, the right thing is on the way.

Whether you seek an Old Covenant truth that still stands available to us today or need a precious promise of the New Covenant, our Father, the owner and operator of the Heavenly General Store, has provided it all. If it's in His Word, it's ready for pick-up.

Such is Kingdom living.

In the Gospels Jesus used many parables to describe the Kingdom of God. He likened it to such things as a precious pearl, a fig tree, a man who sows good seed, a grain of mustard seed, leaven, a treasure, a net, and oil lamps. These stories become relevant for us today as we study them to learn how to live in the Kingdom. We only have to appropriate the power of God's Word in order to enter into Kingdom living here on earth. Besides the benefits of that study, we gain the assurance of an eternity in Heaven with God and our loved ones who are already there.

Kingdom living begins the moment we open the door of our hearts to King Jesus and invite Him into our lives. From that point, we become citizens of Heaven. It may still be a while before we see those streets of gold and mansions on the hilltops, but they belong to us already. That fact alone is reason for rejoicing!

In Romans 14:17, we are told that *"the Kingdom of God is righteousness, and peace, and joy in the Holy Ghost."* Righteousness is being in right standing with God. That happened to me the Christmas I was eight years old. I knelt in front of our little manger scene under the Christmas tree and asked Jesus into my heart. Though my young heart and mind didn't yet understand everything this meant, at that moment I became the righteousness of God in Christ (II Corinthians 5:21). Then as I grew physically, it was my responsibility to get into His Word and to listen to godly teachers who would help me grow spiritually.

In our family trio, The Macs, my husband Dennis, our daughter Stacie, and I sang a song entitled "I Came to Love You Early." This song speaks about accepting the Lord at a young age and how that changes what might have been. It is our testimony song. Stacie came to the realization that she needed Jesus when she was only four years old! I am so thankful for parents who took me to a church that taught the Word of God and I was able to pass on that legacy of knowledge and truth to Stacie.

The Bible came alive to me as soon as I could walk, talk, and sing. The Bible stories I learned in Sunday School and Junior Church were the foundation of my faith. Such things as the courage of the three Hebrew children in the fiery furnace who wouldn't bow down to an idol (Daniel 3), or Queen Esther who stood up for her people even at the risk of her own death (Book of Esther). The compassion of the good Samaritan (Luke 10), and the tenacity of the Apostle Paul in reaching out to bring people to the Lord in his travels and through his letters. All these things built a desire to tell the old, old story of Jesus and His love. I'm glad Dennis and I both learned the basics of faith early and taught them to our daughter because, in the decades that have followed, we have found that Kingdom living is based on making the Word of God final authority in our life. The Word of God contains within itself the power to bring about whatever we need on this earth. But we can't just read it once in a while, or hear it expounded on for an hour on Sunday mornings. We need to feed on the Word daily, get it down into our hearts, let it renew our minds, and then speak it into everyday situations. That is what *Kingdom Corner Connection* is really about: encouraging you to spend enough time with God to know Him and to live well in His Kingdom.

I've experienced the power of God's Word many times in my life. At our lowest point, walking through the valley of the shadow of death felt like more than we could bear. But from the first moment when Dennis and I received news that Stacie had been diagnosed with lymphoma cancer until she went Home to Heaven, God's peace quietly flowed in, flooded our souls and spirits, and pulled us up out of the valley (Philippians 4:7). I never could have imagined the wonderful peace that folded around Dennis and me the day Stacie went to Heaven at the age of 36.

Both my parents were already there, so I'd been through that kind of pain and grief before. But Stacie was our only child. Still, with such love and care, our Shepherd led us through that valley and took us on a sweet journey to the exact place He wanted us to be. Was it easy? Still isn't some days. But we've made it day by day.

I Will Not Fear: A Chosen Life is our testimony book. It has touched many people since it was published in 2013. That I was able to write it was amazing to me. It is my prayer that whatever valleys my readers face, the hope and joy that run through its pages will overflow and bring faith in the place of fear. The peace of God is truly beyond understanding, but it is very real. Trust me. I know.

When I'm working, especially outdoors, and I feel like I'm so tired and can't move another inch, I make myself say, "The joy of the Lord is my strength!" (Nehemiah 8:10) The most recent vivid example of this was after Dennis retired from working 39 years in education. We had moved, and I was unloading the U-haul truck into a storage unit all by myself. Dennis had had to leave and go to our property to take delivery of our little barn. I imagine it was pretty funny to see and hear me shouting those words as I trudged across the parking lot, lugging yet another piece of my life to be stored away for a season. I really did shout, "His joy is my strength!" as I trudged along carrying my heavy loads. I sang about the joy, joy, joy, joy, down in my heart, even though I had to gasp every note.

When I "hit the wall" as I call it, physically or spiritually, that's when I must sing. Just between me and God.

I have learned that every so often I need to stop whatever it is I *think* I have to finish *right now* (which is why I hit walls in the first place), and sit down to rest. More often than not, the Holy Spirit brings a song to me, and it bubbles up inside me like a stopped-up fountain. Joy springs forth from my heart, and my mouth is filled with praise.

The Imperials used to sing a song called "Praise the Lord" based on the scripture about how the Lord inhabits the praises of His people. That song, and one by the Martins called "In the Presence of Jehovah" helped me realize the power of praise. When the term first became popular, I wasn't into "praise and worship" music as I perceived it. All I heard was repetitive phrases, and even if they were straight from the Bible, singing the same thing over and over 42 times did not put me in an attitude of praise! However, through those two songs I learned to praise Him and use music to enjoy His presence in ways I had not experienced before.

What the sacrifice of praise means to me is this: When I don't feel like singing, I do it anyway. When I "turn my eyes upon Jesus," His wonderful presence fills me up and spills over, bringing peace and strength in a supernatural way.

Books and music have always been a part of my life. I believe God planned it that way. Dennis and I will continue on with what the Lord has given us to do, writing books and composing and recording songs. No, our original plan for life didn't happen the way we thought it would. And circumstances still may change, but at this season, oh, how we enjoy Kingdom living! We know it's worth the pursuit to continually grow and learn how to live life in the Kingdom and to stay in the presence and plan of the God we serve. Our desire is to share this place God has given us with people He brings across our path. We will carry out our Kingdom assignment here in our valley, providing a place of rest for family, friends, neighbors. We'll even share our books and songs and all the things our glorious God has made available to His kids, with visitors to the local General Store!

We want to show His love and the power of His Word through our stories and songs. Since we are already in this "re-fire-ment" season, we believe we are where we are supposed to be for the days or years until we move to Heaven. So, we will stay where He has put us, doing what He's called us to do, until He comes again. There, we will live forever in our Heavenly Home, where our Father, Jesus, our precious family, and so many wonders await.

Chapter Two

———————◆———————

Kingdom Unshakable

In the early summer of 1966, I was a carefree ten-year-old, with a busy stay-at-home mom, a strong and caring daddy who read to me, and a brother who just smiled and graciously allowed me to shadow him and his friends. I was the only girl my age on the block. We went to church every Sunday morning, Sunday night, and Wednesday night. I looked forward to being a sixth grader at Central Park Elementary School.

We had finished eating supper on our screened front porch. Dad had stepped out on the stoop to gaze at the ominous green sky filled with rotating clouds. He commented on the muggy stillness of the humid evening. Then the blaring tornado sirens split the air. Dad turned around, wrenched open the screen door, and rushed back inside. He yelled at my brother David and me to grab our pets and hurry to the basement.

As I looked for my cat, Mom took the stairs two at a time to make sure windows were open upstairs. I knew that open windows would stabilize the pressure caused by a tornado and possibly save the house from exploding. Dad was a weather buff and taught us the things he knew were important for us to know living where tornadoes were commonplace.

Dad grabbed a few things from his desk, while my brother collared his dog and Mom helped me corner the frantic cat. Then we filed downstairs to our basement living area. Dad turned on the TV in the corner to the newscast so we would be able to follow the path of the storm. Mom shoved an old metal-topped table into a corner and we all six huddled together underneath its shelter; two adults, two kids, and two pets, one of which did not want to be there. My cat leapt from my arms and ran to his own corner. I tried to follow him, but both parents prevented me from moving, assuring me he would be fine.

The TV weatherman disappeared, black and white dissolving into total darkness with the pop of disconnected power lines. But we didn't need to see the report anymore. We heard it coming. The sound of a thousand trains rumbled in the distance, then propelled across our roof in a deafening roar. The house shook on its foundation.

It seemed like an hour to my child's mind, but in a few minutes the horrible sound and shaking of the tornado and the rattling of windows and doors stopped. Dead silence filled our ears. One by one we crawled out of our shelter and slowly climbed the basement stairs. I looked around and called my cat's name, and was thrilled to see him peek out from underneath the workbench. He wasn't ready to be held. He dodged my arms and meowed sharply as I reached for him, but at least he darted ahead up the steps.

Mom and Dad told us to stay in the kitchen while they slowly walked from room to room upstairs and down. Thankfully, they soon reported back to David and me that there was no visible damage to be seen from the inside. We all walked over to the open back door and stepped onto the screened-in porch. I'd never seen anything like it. Peering out the screen door, I saw trees, shaken by the winds and uprooted, scattered across our yard. Electric lines sparked and danced like beheaded black snakes still fighting for life. The air and sky had transformed from the thick, still pre-storm green, to the clear deep blue of a summer evening. I cried in relief when I saw our tree house still intact, nestled between the branches of the big tree behind our garage.

Soon, the horizon glowed orange-red as the sun set as if it was just another ordinary day. But it wasn't an ordinary day in Topeka, KS. It was June 8, 1966, the day the capital city was sliced in half by a two-mile-wide twister.

Growing up in Kansas, I had experienced many tornado warnings, but this was the closest I came to being the victim of one. I've never felt the shaking power of an earthquake or the devastating prolonged winds of a hurricane, but I imagine the terror is much the same as that day in Topeka. I am so grateful that my family was spared the destruction that many of our friends and neighbors had to deal with. The park where we played was littered with trees. None were left standing. There used to be two ponds where we fished and floated homemade boats. One pond was completely gone, mysteriously sucked up into the funnel cloud leaving a gaping hole, now filled with tree branches.

Central Park grade school was made of red brick, four stories tall. But when we arrived the next day to see how it fared, there was a gaping hole where my first and fourth-grade classes had been. Mom was president of the PTA that year, so she had a tough job ahead. The duties of cleaning up, rebuilding, and starting over for many families, businesses, and schools, assured that things would be very different for the citizens of Topeka for several years to come.

God's Word tells us in Hebrews 12 that when we are shaken by circumstances here on earth, we can be the hope the world needs to overcome those things that shake us to our core. I love the Message translation here. It first refers to the heroes of the faith listed in chapter 11, and the way they paved the pathway for our faith walk and now cheer us on from the Heavenly bleachers. By studying what they did, we can know what to do when our faith is shaken by circumstances. Jesus, too, is our example. What are they telling us? Don't give up, finish our assignments, and have faith in God no matter what.

Next, chapter 12 talks about God's discipline. I discovered that in the original Greek, this word means "training." We train our kids to obey, because we know what disobedience could mean.

They could be hurt or worse. Dad would never have left me on the front porch in that tornado. He commanded me to get my cat and run to the basement. I could have refused and gone out to play never realizing what was coming. But he trained me, not only to know about tornadoes in Kansas and what to do, but to do what he said, when he said it, because he loved me and didn't want me to get hurt.

The children of Israel felt the terrible trembling of the mountain when God spoke and gave Moses the Ten Commandments. They felt the earthshaking rumble of the ground and were afraid of what was happening. But as Hebrews 12 shows us, we have a totally different experience with the Voice of God. We are citizens of the Kingdom. We have a new covenant that gives us right-standing with God because of Jesus and what He did for us on the cross of Calvary. We should obey God's Word, but we don't need to fear His Voice.

Hebrews 12 goes on to say that we will feel the shaking during the last days. In verses 26 and 27, the Message translation says this: *"His Voice that time shook the earth to its foundations; this time, He's told us quite plainly, He'll also rock the heavens: 'One last shaking, from top to bottom, stem to stern,' ...that means a thorough housecleaning, getting rid of all the historical and religious junk so that the unshakable essentials stand clear and uncluttered."* One last shaking will occur, but as citizens of the Kingdom we have no fear because we will escape the destruction to come at the

Judgment. Whether you believe this or not, it is going to shake, rattle, and roll in the end. But then comes a new Heaven and new earth. And eternity.

This is why I love my Kingdom Corner. Taking a specified time, not necessarily the same time and place every day, but somewhere, sometime, to dig into the Bible and search out the amazing stories and truths found in those pages. The Word of God is a living, breathing entity, filled with power! His Word is available to every citizen of the Kingdom, but we have to make the time to turn to Him and His Word. In shaky times and situations God's Word is our greatest stability.

This passage in Hebrews goes on to tell us why: *"Do you see what we've got? An Unshakable Kingdom! And do you see how thankful we must be? And not only thankful, but brimming with worship, deeply reverent before God."* This is a good reminder to me personally what praise, worship, and thanksgiving is all about. God has given us everything! How can we not be thankful and praise Him for it? Yet, when we are shaken, we too often forget this.

The shaking going on in our world is escalating. Every time we turn on the news, we hear about diseases and pandemics, natural disasters, rioting, political unrest, and an ever-widening divide between citizens of all nations. I believe we Kingdom citizens are called to listen to God's Voice in the midst of everything else we hear. His Voice will block out the rest of the world's noise, if we heed

His Word and the still, small Voice of the Holy Spirit. And as open windows help to alleviate the pressure caused by nature's destructive winds, our open ears to the Word of God help alleviate the pressures we face in life. The devil is out there roaring, waiting for every opportunity to steal, kill, and destroy anyone who will listen to him and follow him. He knows his time is short and he is raging and stirring up trouble wherever he can.

We must stand firm as the world's connection to the Unshakable Kingdom. We do this by staying close to Him, clothed in the Armor of God. Those of us who have made Jesus the Lord of our lives possess the stability that people of this world so desperately need. The power and grace given to us is more than sufficient for God to use as a solid anchor for those living in this shaking, breaking world.

You can be a willing vessel through whom God can channel his love and grace to those who are ready to topple over in this shaky and destructive world in which we live. What our fellow man needs right now are willing hands and strong stable voices, sharing God's love to those in physical and spiritual need. This is our calling as citizens of the Unshakable Kingdom.

Chapter Three

◆

Kingdom Keepers

I love that during His time on earth Jesus was a storyteller. Vast crowds gathered on the green hills of Galilee, or lined its seashore, to hear the Master Storyteller weave truths into stories about the Kingdom of God. The Bible calls these stories parables, and Jesus used this method often to teach the people about Who He was and where He came from. There are many parables in the Gospels, but one subject kept coming up. Jesus used many different examples to demonstrate its importance. He wanted the people to understand better what the Kingdom of God is like so they could learn how to enter and live there while still here on earth.

I chose to format this book in three parts because it's essential to understand the Kingdom before going on to establish a physical "corner" and discover the connection to be found there. The first thing needed is to become a citizen of the Kingdom of God by giving your life to the Lord and receiving the sacrifice Jesus provided on the cross. But Kingdom living is so much more than making that first decision.

The parables Jesus shared during His time on earth, as well as by Biblical apostles and modern-day pastors, proclaim the many benefits of living in the Kingdom: forgiveness, righteousness, peace, joy and guidance from the Holy Spirit, healing, and provision, to name a few. We can have all those blessings if we follow the laws of our new Kingdom.

In my *Tresia* book series, I named a group of characters "Kingdom Keepers." Some of these characters lived in the "Earthen Realm," and because they believed, they were also citizens of a higher realm. They were given Kingdom assignments to carry out while still living on earth. Another group of Kingdom Keepers was made up of what I called "Messengers," angel-like beings from the "Garden Realm," who were assigned duties in the Earthen Realm and in the skies between the realms.

The Messenger I want to tell you about is the Keeper of the Vanguards. This is a character that first came from my childhood and was brought back to my mind by a couple of books I read. In one book, the main character had a special name she called God. In the other, the main characters asked God if He had a special name for them. These two questions spoke directly to my heart. The same way I hope and pray certain concepts in my books speak to others.

Before I go further, I want to say that anything we read from human authors, no matter how much an idea may resonate with us at the time of reading, must be weighed against the Word of God. There are plots these days, especially in certain genres, that teeter on the edge of Biblical truth at best, and

fly off the cliff at worst. Sometimes an author spec-
ulates about something "spiritual" that could offend
some readers or lead them away from God's Truth
instead of pointing to it. I never want to do that.

However, I like Christian authors and genres
that make me think and stretch my view of how
God works. I am usually very clear in my spirit
when an idea is not just a different way of looking
at possibilities, but a concept that can cause people
to stumble in their walk with God.

My favorites? The Chronicles of Narnia by
C. S. Lewis, are a series of books I've read over
a dozen times. They were the main inspiration for
my love of the genre. I love thinking about Jesus
as Aslan, an untamed Lion who is wise and loving, yet demands respect and obedience. There are
so many spiritual truths in those books, and that is
what I aspire to do in my writing.

Even in some secular books, I have caught
glimpses of God's character and spiritual truths.
Classic authors have penned some of my favorites,
too. There is room for other opinions, but we must
weigh the things that fill our time and our minds,
and do what the Holy Spirit leads us to do.

The two books which asked about names made
me think. I began to pray about it. What personal
name would I give the Lord? I came up with Chief.
A portion of The Song of Solomon 8:14 popped
into my mind, "the chief among ten thousand to her
soul." I liked that! Since that day, I usually greet the

Lord in the morning with "Good morning, Chief!" I think He likes it, too.

When I asked the Lord what name He calls me, a name I hadn't thought about for years came up in my heart. Wanmaya, my Camp Fire Girls Indian name! I couldn't remember what it meant, so I began to research it in the Cherokee language. This brings me to another story.

The reason we moved to the mountains of Western North Carolina, is that we found our church in the town of Cherokee. It was definitely a God thing, so I wondered if there was a connection to this new line of thinking about the name God calls me. I was shocked and delighted to find that one interpretation of the name Wanmaya is, "Charged with Kingdom Power." I was so excited about this discovery that when I needed a character at the end of the last book in my *Tresia* series, I named her Wanmaya, Keeper of the Vanguards. Vanguards were the prayer warriors in the Earthen Realm, assigned to go ahead of the young ones with powerful "Wind Words" of prayer. The grandmother and aunt to the main character in my books were mighty Vanguards. (These two characters are why many adults have read and enjoyed the books, and shared them with the children in their lives. They, too, pray for those precious children.)

The *Tresia* series are the books I always wanted to write. I thought if I could write a story for middle-grade readers that would make them want to finish reading under the covers with a flashlight long after they were supposed to be asleep (like I used to do), I would be a fulfilled author.

The *Tresia* stories, created in my God-given imagination, had many connections to my own life, such as the story of Wanmaya. That's why the tag line under my name on my website reads: "Kingdom Keeper, Vanguard, and Wielder of Wind Words." In spiritual terms, that means I have a Kingdom assignment to write books, I'm a fierce prayer warrior, and I use my spiritual armor and weapons of warfare in battling for those I love.

While I'm in the midst of writing a book, I always have my "Kingdom Corner" time first. That is when I receive inspiration directly from the Word of God and the Holy Spirit. Your Kingdom Corner time can do the same for you, no matter what your assignment is. Sometimes I receive an idea or inspiration that I think is something brand new. I didn't realize at the time I wrote the *Tresia* series that Kingdom Keepers was a Biblical concept! In my research for writing this chapter, I was amazed as I studied this in the Bible using several translations.

Translations of the Bible are also something that bears a few words of caution. I enjoy reading the "versions" or "paraphrases" for enjoyment. Many read like a novel and make portions of the Bible exciting and easy to follow. But even some that "call themselves" translations are not true translations from the Greek and Hebrew of the original text. When I want to study the Bible, especially a certain book, passage or verse, I turn to the translations which use the original languages. I also consult the writings of the Biblical scholars who have studied the scriptures in those languages. There is plenty of information out there to help you decide the right Bible for you.

I made a list of "Keepers," and there are at least twenty! (In the "Connect Points" at the end of Part I, I have included several titles and references, from different translations, versions, and paraphrases. Look them up for a great Bible study.) I was delighted to find that my "Kingdom Keeper" characters are in good company!

If you spend time in the Word and in prayer, and truly seek God's will for your life, the Holy Spirit will reveal your Kingdom Keeper assignment. Finding your place and job in the Kingdom may take time. Don't be discouraged if you are in a season of growth. At first, you may struggle to know what your assignment is, let alone get started on it. Those times can bring frustration, confusion, and strife, but beware. The devil will take your emotions and try to get you to quit trying. DON'T EVER QUIT! Keep in the Word. Keep praying. Keep seeking. Stay focused. One of my favorite go-to songs in times of questions and waiting, says, "Turn your eyes upon Jesus. Look full in His wonderful face. And the things of earth will grow strangely dim, in the light of His Glory and Grace." Music, anointed by the Holy Spirit to usher us into the presence of God, is a powerful weapon against the devil. He hates it. So, when he tries to trip you up and turn your life in the wrong direction, make a joyful noise and sing! God loves to hear us sing.

Remember, it may take many years of preparation to discover exactly where God wants you to be and what He wants you to do. You may know in general, but God is a God of details, and He has an exact niche prepared for you. I really hadn't thought much about being a writer until I left my library director job to be my mother's full-time caregiver. I had written hundreds of library-related articles and newsletter columns over the years, and even a few newspaper features. But writing those never felt like my calling.

Listening to my mom tell stories of her childhood and the area where she grew up, planted the seeds of my first book, *Dawn of Day*. She was proud of our family heritage, and told me one day that she thought I should write about it. So I did. Not because I wanted to write historical fiction, but because I wanted to do it for Mom, and I felt like God would honor that. I waited too long for her to enjoy the book while she was still here on earth, but I have a feeling she has read it in Heaven.

Then I had another genre writing detour with the memoir of my daughter, Stacie. I knew I had to write this testimony and memoir book first. The Narnia-type books had always been the story of my heart. Not that my first two books weren't also stories of my heart. They had to be. My heart was filled with love and honor for my mother and my daughter. I wanted to tell their stories. But even during those detours in other genres, my writing identity was enlarging and becoming more defined. I don't think the *Tresia* series would be the stories they are if I hadn't written the other two books first. I needed to grow as a writer before I could write what I am called to write. Even this book is related to the *Tresia* books in that the term "Kingdom Corner" is a concept from those stories, and I wanted to write this book to encourage readers to find that same connection I have found.

Have faith in God and the plan He has for you. Tell Him your desires, but do what He tells you to do, even if it's not exactly what you want or planned to do right now. This process requires spending time with Him on a regular basis, digging into His Word, applying it to your life, and acting on it. That includes speaking His Word out loud so you can hear it—and so can the devil. In Romans 10:17 the Bible says, "Faith comes by hearing and hearing by the Word of God." When you say the Word you want to come to pass, you send that Word into the atmosphere where its power is released. It's not enough to just read your Bible, pray a few minutes a day, and attend church once a week. God has so much more for each of us if we take the time to find all the promises, secrets, and mysteries of His Kingdom.

I believe, and it's been my experience, that the journey itself is as exciting as reaching the destination. As I said in the previous chapter, at this season of life Dennis and I are exactly where we are supposed to be, doing what God has called us to do. It has been quite a ride! Every step of the way we've come closer to our destination and the fulfillment of our vision. Many assignments had to be accomplished at different stages in our journey, and they all brought growth in our spiritual lives. I can say without a shadow of doubt, God has used every place He's led us, and all the things He had for us to do, to bring us to this place and this retirement season's assignment. Even in what the devil tried to use to end us, walking through the valley of the shadow of death with Stacie, God took us through, and used it to give us a testimony of faith over fear. Every step made us stronger and more dependent on each other and our individual walk with God, as well as bringing us closer to Him as a couple.

Anyone can be a Kingdom Keeper. The purpose of what we do now, our Kingdom assignments, is to keep the Kingdom of God alive and vibrant, so that when we tell others about it, the Kingdom can increase. As citizens and believers, we all are Kingdom Keepers with divine assignments. If you allow him to, God will use every part of your life experience, your education, jobs, family, joys and successes, heartbreaks, strengths, even your weaknesses. He weaves together each piece of the journey and makes your story a lasting legacy, strong and durable, as well as something that will be used for service in the Kingdom and for others.

Give the Master Storyteller each chapter of your life's journey. He will bring you to the place where you can know and fulfill the individual assignment He always had planned for you.

Chapter Four

———————◆———————

Kingdom Keys

Somewhere in the deep dark recesses of my storage building, is a cardboard box probably labeled, "K.K." for knick-knacks. Inside, is a quart-sized mason jar filled with keys. Some are very old skeleton keys that I've unearthed over the years. I like how they look, so I always save them. Most are keys to the places I've lived, houses where my family members have lived, and other various buildings we kept locked. There's probably a key to most of my former vehicles, and even a few tiny keys that locked away secrets in jewelry boxes or cedar chests. Old padlock keys? At least a dozen, I'm sure. But most of those old keys only unlock things I no longer need or possess. The jar makes an interesting knick-knack to set on a shelf, but there is not one single key in there that does me any good whatsoever. I have brand new keys that unlock the places and things to which I need access now.

When we become citizens of the Kingdom, after we accept Jesus as Lord of our lives, we are given brand new tools and "weapons" that enable us to live well, even while still living in this Earth. But unless we use and understand the new tools God has provided, they do us no good. God calls these tools and resources Keys to the Kingdom.

Matthew 16:19, CEV, says it this way. "I will give you the keys to the Kingdom of Heaven, and God in Heaven will allow whatever you allow on earth. But He will not allow anything you don't allow." Most other versions say "whatever you bind on earth, will be bound in Heaven and whatever you loose on earth, will be loosed in Heaven." I had a hard time understanding that verse until I read it in the Contemporary English Version.

As Kingdom citizens, we have been given everything we need to unlock the power of God. We should be doing things that the world doesn't understand, things they can't explain. We have the keys that will unlock the mysteries and secrets of the Kingdom. These keys are for our use as citizens, such as healing and provision. Our keys also unlock miracles, knowledge, and wisdom. The world needs our Kingdom Keys. They are to be used to show people the resources available to anyone who comes into the Kingdom. We have in our hands the keys that will help them want to become a citizen of the Kingdom. But before we can show the world, we have to know how to use them for ourselves.

The disciples saw and experienced Jesus perform many miracles, from healing the sick, multiplying the bread, and walking on water, to raising the dead. What Jesus taught was that these miracles were Kingdom Keys. He used them to unlock healing, deliverance, provision, joy, peace, and authority over the devil. Jesus demonstrated the way the Kingdom works, so in the same way, we could learn how to use the keys we have been given.

The first key I want to talk about is the Key of Authority. As Matthew 16:19 says, we have the authority to ask for, expect, and allow healing, provision, and deliverance to come to us here on earth, because those things come from Heaven. We also have the authority to not allow sickness, lack, and captivity to any addiction or habit that comes from the devil because none of those things are allowed in Heaven. That is much easier for me to understand than "binding and loosing" as some other versions call it.

When Adam and Eve sinned in the Garden of Eden, they gave their God-given authority to satan. But God still had a plan. His plan of salvation through the life, death, and resurrection of Jesus, provided that when we become citizens of the Kingdom, authority on earth is given back to us! Authority to use the Name of Jesus is ours as well. The Key of Authority unlocks everything we need down here. The key to your house gives you authority and access to your home, just as this Kingdom key gives us authority and access to all the resources of Heaven! So act like it! Have the confidence to bring Heaven to Earth in the Name of Jesus. With the Keys to the Kingdom, we can have the Blessings of Heaven now!

The term, "God is in control" has been used over and over when something bad happens and we don't understand or know what to do about it. The thought that no matter what, "God is in control" seems to help us feel better. But another Key to the Kingdom is the Key of Control. God has given *us* control over our own bodies and minds. We can't always control the hardships we face, sickness, lack, or a torment in a mind or soul, but we can control how we react to them by giving our bodies to God, and renewing our minds with His Word. That doesn't mean that tough times don't exist, but if we seek out a specific scripture that speaks into that particular situation, that Word brings life, health, strength or peace into that circumstance. The spoken Word of God renews our minds and changes circumstances.

My pastor shared a story about a neighbor of his who gave him a key to his storage building. Inside were tools and equipment that would provide whatever he needed to do a job. But if the key was never used, if the walk over to the building was never made, the door never unlocked, all that provision that would help him accomplish his job sat in the building unused. The choice had to be made to use the key and access what was needed. It was available, but it still required action to acquire the provision.

In the story of the prodigal son (Luke 15:11-32), the younger son wanted his inheritance right then. The father said it was his, and he took it and left. After a few months of partying and wasting his father's money, the younger man realized that he'd made a huge mistake. He decided to return to his father's house and be a servant, because even his father's servants were in better shape than he was in the pig pen. But as soon as he returned and the father saw his son, he ran to him, and treated him like the son that he had been all along. Most people know that part of the story.

The older son became angry and confronted his father, saying that he was the one who stayed and continued to work for him. He never took the inheritance that was offered, though it was also available to him at that time. He resented his father for never killing the fat cow for him and giving him a party with his friends!

The father's answer to the older brother demonstrates what our Heavenly Father has provided for us. He said that all he possessed had belonged to both sons from the day they were born into the family. Though one took the inheritance and squandered it, the money was his to do with as he pleased. The father told his other son, "Don't you know that you are always with me and all I have is yours?" Both sons had the key to the inheritance. One took it and used the inheritance for his own pleasure. The older brother blamed the father, but it was he (the son) who never took advantage of what was available to him all the time. Keys can be used wrongly, or not at all. But they are available either way.

God has given his family the resources of Heaven. You have the keys. Do you need healing or provision from Heaven's supply house? Take it now. How? We take control, authority, and power over a bad situation down here, by putting the Word of God in our mouths and saying it out loud. Speak the solution, not the problem. Speak the Word out loud, read it slowly, meditate on what it says you have. Do this until the truth of that Word builds your faith, floods your heart and mind, and you know it's yours. The Bible says that God calls those things that are not as though they are. That's how we operate, too. It's not denying that a bad situation exists, it's denying its right to stay in our lives.

In Matthew 8, Jesus didn't deny there was a storm raging when the disciples woke him because they were so frantic and afraid they would die. He just spoke to the storm and it calmed. If we speak to our storms in the same way, with faith and no fear, we can experience that same peace. The outcome may not be exactly what we expected or wanted, but if we trust in the Word of our loving Heavenly Father, we can rest assured that He will be right there with us, through the storm and beyond. His Word says that He works everything for our good, whether something in life takes us through a valley, or leads us to a mountaintop.

I have a motto: If it's good, it's from God, if it's bad, it's from satan. We live in a fallen world and the devil is always roaring about! We make the choice to listen to his noise and let him trample over us, or we tell him to go to hell! I do that often because that's where he belongs, and I enjoy telling him so. The Bible says he's under our feet, and I usually give him a good stomp, too! (I got all that from a preacher friend, so it's OK.)

I've been through a lot of storms in my life, but I've learned to speak to those storms in faith and authority. They may leave some debris behind, like missing loved ones for a little while, but His peace remains—the peace that truly does pass understanding. There is never any condemnation from my Father, even if I didn't understand and do everything I could have done, or if I let my emotions get out of control. The prodigal son and his brother both discovered their father's compassion, forgiveness, and love even when they made wrong decisions and failed to use the keys their inheritance provided the way the father meant for them to be used. Either way, the Father loves us and will work it out for our good. His plan for each of us is amazing.

In my *Tresia* books, I wanted to introduce to my young readers, the concept of using our Keys to the Kingdom. During the pre-writing time to plot and make notes, I had made a chart for all three books in the series to make sure I could carry out what I wanted to do. It's called *Trinity Tales of Tresia* because I wanted to have three separate, but related, tales in each book. Kind of a three-for-one deal. In order to do that, I had to plan and write out at least some sort of plot for each book. I'm not a plotter in the actual writing process, because I like to let the Spirit flow! But a little planning is very helpful in the beginning. Many hours of Kingdom

Corner time go into this process before I even begin writing.

The mountain valley, where we live now is known for its gem mining. We were looking for property and had already visited this area several times before I began the *Tresia* series. I had seen the many gem mines scattered across the valley and I was intrigued. That inspired me to have my illustrator draw an area marked Gem Mines on the map in the first book. I wanted one of the tales to have a journey that included the kids going into the mines. I hadn't planned on the "keys" concept to come in where it did, but that's how the Holy Spirit co-writes with me. I may have just read about, or heard a sermon on, the Keys to the Kingdom. Most of the time, the seeds I need for the story are planted in my heart, or brought to my remembrance, during Kingdom Corner time.

In the first tale of the second book, while the two twelve-year-old main characters explore the Gem Mines, David spots a small silver box, half-hidden in the underground stream that runs through the middle of the mine. He opens it and finds three jewel keys, each carved from a single ruby, sapphire, or amethyst. These three keys unlock a door, a gate, and the power of the special gift they had been given at the beginning of their journeys—an extraordinary umbrella. Through the three tales in the book, the kids learn how to use the jewel keys to unlock the power they need for the moment. Sound familiar?

Learn how to use your keys. Dig out the knowledge contained in the Word of God just for you. God's Word is life, truth, and freedom. Time spent in your Kingdom Corner seeking the truths the Holy Spirit wants to show you, will supply everything you need. Time with God is the key to learning how to bring Heaven's resources to earth when you need them. Keys aren't mere knick-knacks. They are yours as a Kingdom citizen, and they work if you learn how to use them.

The Keys to the Kingdom represent our freedom. We can be free from fear and the limitations of living here on earth. We are free to access Heaven and bring its resources to help us accomplish our Kingdom assignments now. Kingdom Keys contain the Truths of God and His Word.

John 8:31-32, NKJV says, *"If you abide in My Word, you are My disciples indeed. And you shall know the Truth, and the Truth shall set you free."*

Chapter Five

———————◆———————

Kingdom Beyond Time

When my daughter Stacie was a young girl, my cousin Jill introduced us to a white sled- dog breed, known for its smile. The day we met Jill's canine Samoyed companion Rachael, Stacie fell in love with the dog and the breed. She wanted one right away, but she didn't get one for several years.

By her sophomore year in high school, nothing else was on her Christmas list. We opted for a brand new puppy. We'd already received several cards graced with photos of an entire litter as they peeked above red and green baskets decked in bright shiny bows. The adorable little balls of snowy fluff with shiny black eyes and mouths that curled up in irresistible grins, were known as Christmas pups, the perfect holiday gift.

The decision was made. We all wanted to add a Samoyed to our family. We researched where to find Samoyed pups for sale, and decided on a breeder in Kansas City, only an hour and a half away. Kansas City was our usual family Christmas lights and shopping destination, so we all three jumped in the car a few days before the holiday to make our yearly trip to the Country Club Plaza, an area known for its Christmas lights and decorations.

But first, we went in search of our new dog.

When we arrived at the breeder's home, he opened a door in the back of the house and we stepped into a room full of cottony pups, rolling around and over each other. How could we resist the cuteness? Stacie stood for a moment looking at her many choices. She hadn't made a move toward any of them, when one little pup teetered over to her and rested its head on her tennis shoe. The puppy chose Stacie, not the other way around. Stacie reached down and cuddled the pup in her arms. Not a word was needed. We knew which puppy was going home with us. The breeder had told us that if we didn't want a family dog, then we didn't want a Samoyed. He was right. But we did, and she became a member of the family right away.

We named her Guinevere Ariel, from Camelot and Little Mermaid. Her official name was registered in case Stacie decided to breed her later. She didn't. Guinevere was Ginny to us, and she was a joy from day one. The only down side of owning a "Sammie" is the long white hair they shed every year, enough to make a Christmas sweater! I found out after years of brushing and tossing hair that we could have actually sold it to weavers! Our family learned to live with white hair everywhere, in spite of daily brushings and sweepings. We kept several lint rollers around within easy reach!

Ginny was Stacie's dog, and for the next two years, Stacie helped take good care of her...until it was time to leave home for college. Then Ginny became my dog, too. It was uncanny how I could tell Ginny missed having Stacie around through the week, even though our daughter came home almost every weekend. (Praise the Lord!) I could see the wheels turning in Ginny's doggie mind. For the five years Stacie was in college, Ginny and I were constant companions. She was a great traveler and loved to ride in the car, so we took her with us often. When we stopped to walk her, people commented on how beautiful she was, and kids always wanted to pet her. Ginny loved children and senior citizens. She accompanied me and my mom with her dog J.J on our regular trips to the nursing homes to visit my aunts. Both dogs were a hit with patients and staff.

We had Ginny for seven years before pancreatic cancer took her from us. I'll never forget driving to Emporia State University, where Stacie was scheduled to sing in her Senior Recital a few days later, to tell her Ginny was gone. That's the other down side of pet ownership, the emptiness when they leave.

After a few months, we began to think about adopting a rescue dog. Stacie wanted another Samoyed, and I did, too. On the way back from Stacie's first trip to North Carolina to interview for music teaching jobs, we stopped half-way home and adopted our second Samoyed from St. Louis Samoyed Rescue. Tara was the name she already had and we kept it, thinking about the grand white home in *Gone With the Wind.*

Tara was with us twice as long as Ginny, fourteen years, so in doggy years, she was a long-time member of the family. Though they were the same breed, our two Sams were as different as human siblings can sometimes be. Ginny weighed over 80 pounds, but Tara was the runt of her litter, and had been abused, so she started small and thin and was afraid of men. She never grew larger than forty-five pounds, but every pound was filled with love. Dennis won her over quickly.

Both dogs had wonderful personalities. Ginny loved to run at top speed, if she had a big area to do so. She was also quieter vocally. Tara "talked" to us all the time in her whiny language and did more pulling than walking when I'd take her on my walking trail! They had two things in common. If they got off the leash or out of the fence, they both ran off as fast as they could with not a glance behind at the crazy people yelling at them to come back! And they both loved to romp in snow! I have photos of Tara posing in a new foot-high snowfall. About all you can see are her black eyes and her smile!

In many ways, it was harder to lose Tara than it had been to lose Ginny, because we had her so many more years. The hole she left was bigger.

One of my favorite things about being a writer is that it gives me license to use my imagination and create something that may, or may not, be how it is in reality. This is why I so enjoy writing inspirational fantasy fiction. I took that liberty in my *Tresia* series. Along with using family and friends' names for characters, both my Samoyeds are immortalized in the *Tales of Tresia*, as "Winged Beasts." Talking, flying Winged Beasts! I was honored to include some of my friends' pets as Winged Beasts, too. One of my editors also had a white dog named Zion. She is the main canine character in the third book. Several friends' cats also gained their wings in *Tresia*.

In the first book of the series, it is Ginny who ushers the main characters into the Kingdom Beyond Time. Toward the end of the book, they have all had a drink from the "First Well of Kai-ohr," (its name means Life-Light,) and Vince, the main male character, is about to lift the veil that separates them from the other realm.

"He reached his hand up to the veil and drew it back. The brightness spilled over us as the dark curtain lifted.

"Without drinking from the First Well of Kai-ohr," Ginny told us, "humans can't bear the glorious light."

She bounded across to the other side, leaping and jumping. Then she unfurled her wings, soared upward, and looped through the clear blue sky. I had known Samoyeds could smile, but not that they could laugh out loud!

The three of us...followed the diamond trail scattering from Ginny's wingtips. With the same joyous abandon demonstrated by my very own Winged Beast, we laughed and ran through the door into the Kingdom Beyond Time."

A few pages later is a glimpse of our mortal connection to that Kingdom from Gahlay Rahzeen, (the Holy Spirit character whose Name means Revealer of Mysteries.)

"You have already established your own secret places in the Earthen Realm," Gahlay Rahzeen explained. *"During the time you spend in your Kingdom Corners you will discover many secrets, treasures, and mysteries of the Kingdom."*

That's the reason I wanted to write "Kingdom Corner Connection." As I wrote these stories from my own experiences and my God-given imagination, it was my greatest desire that they be exciting and adventurous tales. But it was very important to me that my stories should also contain Truths from God's Word that would resonate with kids and adults alike. I want to help my readers grow in their walk with the Lord and realize the power they have here in the "Earthen Realm," as well as be assured of the glorious future waiting in Heaven, the "Kingdom Beyond Time."

I chose that name because I love that the Kingdom is a timeless place. I believe Time began when God created man, and it will end when the devil is finally out of here and tossed into his fiery eternal home! Time is only a piece of Eternity. When a statement like that lodges in my soul, it usually ends up in a book. This quote is from *A*

Most Remarkable Hat: Book I in the *Trinity Tales of Tresia* series:

> **Three in One carved out**
> **a piece of Eternity.**
> **and We called it Time.**

I don't claim to be a poet, and poetry has never been high on my reading or writing list. But the haiku poetic form worked perfectly for my story. It provided a fun way to give the young characters clues to their adventures, and many of the "Hai-klues" as I call them, were based on Scripture. This last one at the end of the first book was adapted from a teaching I heard about the meaning of time. It fit perfectly. And I think I even got the meter right.

I love reading stories of people whose bodies have clinically died for whatever reason, but their spirits and souls made a trip to Heaven. The stories are eerily familiar in the details of places and things they saw and experienced while out of the body. It certainly makes one think about the possibilities. Though they may have wanted to stay in some cases, the person, a loved one, or Jesus himself, made a decision that they needed to return to earth for a while. Most of these accounts say the person felt as though they had been gone for a long time, but upon returning to their bodies, only minutes had passed here on earth. Maybe that's why I relate to *Narnia* so much and gave *Tresia* the same quality. Time is different there.

When Stacie departed earth in 2012, we learned early on to keep our minds on Heaven. We were given a copy of a book called, *Inside Heaven's Gates* by Rebecca Springer. It has become a favorite, and Dennis and I have both read it multiple times. Another friend and wonderful singer and psalmist, Len Mink, wrote ten "Songs They Sing in Heaven," inspired by Springer's book and the Holy Spirit. The songs on that CD are guaranteed to lift you out of grief. I'm not a fan of "grief therapy," though many tried to get us to seek it out. Some, I know have truly been helped by it and if you need that outlet, then do it. No condemnation from me.

But we had a different kind of therapy. I call it Heaven Therapy. I wrote Stacie's testimony book, *I Will Not Fear: A Chosen Life*, with the main theme of hope for the future, forever with God and our loved ones. We can only have that hope of seeing family and friends again who have already gone before us if we have made Heaven our final destination.

One of my favorite teachings by Rev. Keith Moore is from a series titled, *Victory Over Death*. We first listened to this series on our way home from the service we had for Stacie in Kansas. The Holy Spirit orchestrated our spending some time in Branson, Missouri on our way home, where we "accidently" arrived right after this series ended. Pastor Keith mentioned it in the sermon that day, and we knew it was meant for us. It made all the difference. Even all these years later, the Heaven Therapy we soaked up all the way home still makes me smile. We go back and listen to the series often for a "booster therapy session." Pastor Keith talked about how once a person reaches Heaven he is unaware of the passing of time. This confirmed other things we had been taught and read in the Bible and in accounts of people who had been there and returned.

I told about this experience in Stacie's book. In wonder, we thought about the possibility that once we finally join Stacie again after we depart earth or Jesus comes in the clouds to take us Home to Heaven, we will find Stacie busy doing her Heavenly assignment, whatever that is! I like to think she is still a teacher, only now her students are all the little ones who are waiting for their parents to join them. One of Stacie's friends had a miscarriage, and when she read that in Stacie's book, she told me that she loved that thought and it gave her great comfort.

Pastor Keith gave us a wonderful hope to hang on to when he said that those loved ones who are already in Heaven will pause what they're doing, turn around and see us, and exclaim, "Wow! You're already here!"

How can I not smile at the picture in my mind of my daughter saying those words? I'm sure if her friends are reading this, they would say the same about her expression! I can't wait to see and hear it in person.

Time began with God's first dealings with man in the Garden of Eden. For each of us, becoming a citizen of that Kingdom begins the moment we make Jesus our Lord. Then all the benefits of the Kingdom are ours, even now, here on earth. I have many friends and family listed in my prayer journal who need healing right now. In the natural, doctors have given them little hope of being well and strong again. But I believe we have the key to unlock supernatural healing here and now by believing and standing on the healing scriptures, speaking them out of our mouths, and acting on them. Even medical specialists say that attitude is a huge part of the healing process. If we adopt the attitude that no matter what the doctor report says, we know the Great Physician and He still wants us well, strong, and testifying to His healing power, then we can turn things around.

Even if you end up in Heaven, like my own precious daughter, making the journey in strong faith is the best way to go.

But the best news of all? When Time is done, we will be with Jesus in a brand new body, and the Kingdom Beyond Time will never end.

PART I
The Kingdom

◆

Connect Points

Chapter One: Kingdom Living

Are you a citizen of the Kingdom of God? If not, stop right now and ask Jesus to be your King and Lord of your life.

If you already are a citizen of the Kingdom, take some time and think about or write down, where, when, and how you made that decision. It's always good to remember the experience of meeting Jesus, even if you can't pinpoint a day or time.

List several ways you can practice Kingdom Living. How does Kingdom citizenship affect your daily choices, spiritually, physically, socially, and financially?

Chapter Two: Kingdom Keepers

Why do you think Jesus used parables to teach about the Kingdom? Find and study the passages where He told Kingdom of God parables. Which story speaks the most to you?

Here is a partial list of the Kingdom Keepers in the Bible. The titles are taken from several translations and versions of the Bible; New English Version, Passion Translation, Tree of Life Version, Youngs Literal Translation, The Message, and Amplified Classic Translation.

- Keeper of the wardrobe – NEV / II Kings 22:14
- Keeper of the royal nature preserve, (forest), NEV, King's paradise, YLT – Nehemiah 2:8
- Keeper of the gates, YLT / East Gate, TLV – II Chronicles 35: 15
- Keeper of the house, TLV – Ecclesiastes 12:3
- Keeper of the money box (bag), NEV – John 12:6
- Keeper of souls, PT – Proverbs 24:12
- Keeper of the flock, TLV – 1 Samuel 17:20
- Keeper of service, TLV – Ezekiel 44:8
- Keeper of the field, TLV – Jeremiah 4:17
- Keeper of Israel, TLV – Psalm 121:4
- Keeper of the vineyards, NEV – Song of Solomon 1:6
- Keeper of the threshold, YLT – II Kings 22:4, 23:4, 25:18, I Chronicles 9:19
- Keeper of oracle words, Message – Revelation 1:3
- Keeper of the temple, NEV – Acts 19:35

Can you find more Keepers in the Bible?

Do you have a Kingdom Keeper assignment? If so, write it down or share it with someone.

What steps can you take to begin or continue to fulfill your assignment?

Chapter Three: Kingdom Keys

Go back through the chapter, and write down the principles of the Keys to the Kingdom.

What surprised you most about the keys you have been given to use as a citizen of the Kingdom?

For each key principal you wrote down, journal or think about what that means to you and your circumstances today. How can that principal change your circumstances?

How can you use a Kingdom Key to unlock the answers you need right now?

Chapter Four: Kingdom Unshakable

Have you ever been in a natural disaster that literally shook your surroundings? What emotions came to the surface? Was there someone there to help you deal with the resulting emotions?

Have you ever had a spiritual "shaking" in your life? How did you deal with the emotions it caused? Was there someone or something that helped to stabilize your spiritual life afterwards?

Read Hebrews 12 in several translations and pick the one that speaks to you the most. How does that translation help you to better understand our unshakable Kingdom? What does it say about your role as a stable anchor for the rest of the world?

Write a list of practical things you can do to help stabilize someone you know whose life is shaky right now.

I learned as a child that open windows help with the pressure of a tornado, and that I could trust my dad when he asked me to obey him. I likened that to opening my ears to the Voice inside me, to help with the pressures of life, and that I can trust my Heavenly Father when he asks me to do something. Can you relate a natural experience, like a weather event or emotional trauma that shook your life, to a spiritual lesson you learned from it?

What aspect of being a citizen of the unshakable Kingdom means the most to you? What do you need to develop in your life, so you will be a stable anchor for others in times of trouble?

Chapter Five: Kingdom Beyond Time

If you've had a pet that was or is part of your family, share or write down a special memory of them. You may or may not believe that pets will be in Heaven, but I like to think about it. If you knew you would see a beloved pet again, describe the scene of your reunion.

I talked about books and music that touched my heart in special ways when we experienced loved ones moving to Heaven. Is there a book or song that has done the same for you in your time of need? Go back and read or listen to the words. Be ready to share with someone else who is battling grief, how that author or musician's words have helped you.

Is there a certain verse or passage of Scripture that the Lord has put on your heart when you are missing someone? How have those words given you peace and strength? Write it down and share with a friend.

Imagine what a loved one is doing in Heaven today. How does that image change your grief or sadness? Along with the Scriptures, books, and music, would you add anything else to your own personal "Heaven Therapy" session? Journal about it, or share your thoughts with a friend who needs to hear about the Kingdom Beyond Time.

If you need healing in your body, mind, relationships, finances, or any situation, search out Bible verses that speak to what you need. Keep those key Words in your eyes, your ears, and speak them out loud. This builds your faith for the answer to come. God is faithful!

*"You live in the Earthen Realm, but by choice you are not a citizen of it anymore. You chose to become an adopted child of my Father...Now you will live the **Kingdom** way. Your hat was given to you to help you understand what my Covering of Deliverance has provided for you. Gahlay Rahzeen, (Revealer of Mysteries)...will guide you from this day forward."*

Quote from *Hah D'Var*, (The Word),
Trinity Tales of Tresia, Book I:
A Most Remarkable Hat

PART II

THE CORNER

Cor'ner, *noun*

The interior point where two lines meet; an angle.

An enclosed place; a secret or *retired place.

   * Reti'red, *adjective*

    Secluded from much society or from public notice; private.

    Withdrawn

———————◆———————

> *"Am I not a God near at hand "*
> *"and not a God far off?*
> *Can anyone hide out in a **corner***
> *where I can't see him? "*
> *"Am I not present everywhere,*
> *whether seen or unseen? "*

Matthew 13:51-52 The Message (MSG)

Chapter Six

◆

In My Own Little Corner

As a young girl, the original Rogers and Hammerstein's *Cinderella* was one of my favorite musicals. It was the dream my friends and I talked about—to meet a handsome prince, fall in love, and be swept away to the castle. The music carried me to places in my imagination, just like Cinderella as she sat in her own little corner in her own little chair. It may have been a dark dingy attic, but she could be whatever she wanted to be.

That early scene in the musical may have been a seed of the idea for what I now call my Kingdom Corner. But what I do there was influenced, not by a make-believe fairy tale, but by something I was introduced to at church camp when I was eight years old. I had invited Jesus into my heart the Christmas before. I learned much about the Bible and my Savior at church, but it was only a beginning. When summer rolled around, I was ready for my first camp experience, not only to do the fun activities, but also to learn more about how to be a child of God. The first step in that process was spending time with Him in a quiet place. Camp was the perfect setting to establish that pattern. The first thing we did every morning before breakfast, was find a quiet spot somewhere on the grounds and have our quiet time with the Lord. It was a good beginning to a life-long habit.

Over the years I've had many designated places for my quiet time: a bedroom, an out-of-the-way place in the house, my reading/writing nook, or anywhere outside. The mountains, the ocean, a garden, a porch, sitting on my roof overlooking Kansas golden wheat and green corn fields, all have provided peace and inspiration. I like talking to God in the midst of His beautiful creation.

Since I started writing, my office space has usually doubled as my quiet-time place, especially since I began the *Tales of Tresia* series. That's where I coined the phrase, "Kingdom Corner." Both young and older characters in the books have a special place where they meet with the Holy Spirit character. It's a concept that I hope will cause kids of all ages to want to create a special place for this purpose. And there are added benefits. Most of my story ideas come from spending time in my Kingdom Corner. The Holy Ghost and I collaborate on my stories. He is the perfect writing partner.

In the *Tresia* books, when the connection is made between the Earthen Realm and the Garden Realm, a sparkly blue light appears and the conversation is called Wind Words. It makes for a more interesting story, and I'm not saying God *wouldn't* do something like appear in a sparkly blue light, but usually not. My Kingdom Corner is just a place where I can connect to God and have a conversation in prayer about whatever is on my heart, or

His, that day. The Holy Spirit is an awesome listener. I'm learning to be a better listener, too.

I usually begin with praise, worship, and thanksgiving, and I use music during that time. I already talked about the way I learned to enjoy praise and worship time, by finding anointed songs that speak to my spirit. I admit it. I am particular about the music I listen to, especially in my Kingdom Corner time. Len Mink, our friend who is a lead worshiper (not a worship leader) and songwriter, says that the purpose of praise and worship time is to create an atmosphere for the Word of God to be delivered. That's true in a church service or in our individual time with God. Much of my prayer time and speaking the Word is accompanied by music. When the songs fade, it's time for me to dig into the Word.

At the end of each year, I ask the Lord which specific Biblical book or subject, He wants me to study the following year. I use other writers' books to enhance my study, but those books must agree with the Bible. My yearly study is connected to what I call my "word" for that year. I started this practice in 2011 and have kept it up. Around October, I start noting words that the Lord brings to my attention. By Christmas, I have always known what my word for the New Year will be. (I have listed my "Words of the Year" in the Connect Points section for this chapter.)

After praying, reading, and studying, I close my books. Getting quiet and listening for that still, small Voice inside my heart is the crucial element, one I'm still developing. I ask the Lord what He wants to tell me or show me about what I've read or prayed about. It's not easy to take even five minutes of total silence and focus on the Holy Spirit speaking to me. It takes practice and I am much better at it than I used to be. After a few minutes, I write down what God lays on my heart. Writing things down is an important step for me. If I don't write down my thoughts and especially specific instructions God gives, I can forget them before I get up! And it's good for developing my author skills. I do my best to obey whatever He shows me. If I don't put into practice what I learn, then quiet time is wasted time. But with consistency and obedience, what I gain from my Kingdom Corner time is priceless, and after over fifty years of developing my time with God, it's something I wouldn't give up.

In my last house, I had a cute little room that was both my writing studio and my Kingdom Corner. I was surrounded by books and photos and all things literary. That space was filled with great inspiration. With a retired husband it's been harder, especially since at this time we are between houses and living in a 26-foot camper. Sometimes, we all have to be creative with both our time with God, and accomplishing the assignments He gives us. For now my camper couch, a chair outside, or a walk in the evergreens on our property becomes my Kingdom Corner time. I also have a place in my barn where many of my favorite books are shelved temporarily. It's quiet. But there's no electricity for heating, cooling, or plugging in my laptop, so it's not an option. I won't even mention the bugs...I have sticky bug catchers everywhere.

Many times I wait until later at night when it's quiet, instead of spending time with God in the morning, which I prefer. Finding a balance between honoring my Kingdom Corner time and writing time, and honoring and spending time with Dennis can be a challenge. But we are figuring it out. Both are a priority for us, and I've learned that actual time put aside for each can be flexible. I do whatever I have to do to have my time with God, give Dennis quality time, and keep writing!

Whether you call it a Kingdom Corner or not, my hope is that this section about "The Corner" of your Kingdom living will cause you to want to find a special place and time to meet with God every day. Nothing you can do is more important if you want to find and keep a connection to the Kingdom.

In the first *Tresia* book, the Grandmother and aunt characters use their Kingdom Corners for a special reason:

"Gran eased into her rocking chair and lifted her Book of Covenants to her lap. She'd just talked to her daughter. Both women were honored to be Vanguards, those chosen to go before the battle using their Wind Words as the first line of defense against the enemy. A Vanguard's own family

members were always the first charges assigned to their care."

This is one of the main things I do in my Kingdom Corner. At the front of my prayer journal, I have a list of all my family members, adopted family, and special friends who are like family. The first minutes of my prayer time are devoted to the loved ones on this list.

Do you have a list of loved ones you pray for regularly? When I am in my Kingdom Corner, I am a Kingdom Keeper, Vanguard, and Wielder of Wind Words. You can be, too.

Chapter Seven

———————◆———————

Shop Around the Corner

In 2019, I attended the Rubart Writing Academy. On the pre-Academy survey, we were asked to name our top five movies. I wrote down what I thought were my top five, the ones I watch over and over and never tire of seeing. From the list I submitted, it was determined that my writing identity is that I champion the underdog. However, I wasn't sure that truly was my main identity as a writer. Later, I realized something that hadn't occurred to me when making the original list. I had listed a couple of my favorite movies, but the other three were some of Stacie's favorite movies. Films we watched together over and over. Those precious memories of time spent with my daughter caused me to jump to the conclusion that they were my favorite movies, too.

But for the purpose of this exercise I needed to choose *my* favorites to discover that place in my heart from where my most powerful stories come. What is my identity as an author? The conclusion drawn from my original list was that I champion the underdog. I had never connected that trait to my writing.

How many times do we adopt the likes and dislikes of those we love, even if in our heart of hearts, we disagree or at least would choose differently? I hadn't put enough of myself into my answers. I assumed my memories were right. In this case, it wasn't necessarily a bad thing. My joy in watching them with Stacie made those movies my favorites, too. But my answers for the workshop weren't the real and complete truth. So, I spent some time in my Kingdom Corner thinking about *my* favorite movies and why I watch them over and over, even if all alone. I asked the Lord to reveal to me the difference in my list and Stacie's list.

You may think that movies are not something God is interested in, but it's the same principal I've talked about before. We are citizens of the Kingdom of God and live in that Kingdom simultaneously with our life on earth. Everything we do here affects our Kingdom life. God cares if I watch movies or TV shows or read books that contain plots that are good for my soul and spirit, or not. I know that it would not please the Lord if I watch a movie, TV show, or read a book filled with things the Bible condemns. I didn't used to be as careful about that, but now, I am very selective in my leisure entertainment. I am much more sensitive to the Holy Spirit as I watch, listen, or read. He lives in me, and therefore, He is watching, listening, or reading as well. That knowledge gives me pause in making all decisions, including leisure activities.

I admit that I do watch and read things that may not have much spiritual value, but are strictly for laughs or pure entertainment, figuring out whodunit, or considering the situations people get into so I can seek the Lord on how to help those I encounter in similar circumstances. I think the Lord is OK with that, too. We do still live in this world, and sometimes we need to observe it in order to know what the Kingdom response should be. But we must discern and choose what will relax us, exercise our minds, or give us knowledge the Lord can shed light on—not things that will open the door to the devil and bring his evil into our lives.

My list of favorite movies include: *You've Got Mail*, (with Meg Ryan and Tom Hanks,) *Good-bye Girl* (original with Richard Dreyfuss and Marsha Mason,) *Funny Face* (with Audrey Hepburn and Fred Astaire,) *Brigadoon*, (with Gene Kelly and Cyd Charisse,) and *Mary Poppins*, (original with Julie Andrews and Dick Van Dyke, and recently I added Mary Poppins Returns!) I have watched these five movies at least a dozen times over the years. I watched Mary Poppins the most because I first met her when I was just a girl. Though the language and some situations in a couple of my favorite movies are not ideal, they all tell a story that touches my heart. With Stacie's favorites, it was more about humor and the joy of being together.

With these five movies, I agreed that my writing identity does champion the underdog, but also that I write to share the power of story and music. I can see how all five books I have authored thus far, as well as many blogs and articles, have come from this place, planted deep in my heart and revealed in my writing. I haven't tried it yet, but the exercise would probably work with TV shows I've watched and books I've read. That may be a "Contact Point" I need to do myself after writing this chapter!

Though this exercise was used in a workshop for writers, I think it would work for anybody who is struggling with who they are and what they were created to do. It's a starting place at least. It may be easier for those who work in the creative arts to relate to the concept, such as writers, artists, musicians, actors, etc. But God created us all with a unique plan and purpose. He put into our very being whatever we need for accomplishing that purpose. Therefore, it makes sense that we all have a creative streak. Lately, those of us with an artistic bent have been referred to as "Creatives." But creativity is present in whoever we are and whatever we do. God put it there.

I wish I had learned my writing identity much earlier than I did. However, in God's usual loving and all-knowing fashion, He guided my writing over the last decade to follow that purpose. Now in my mid-sixties, I see His imprint on my life and writing. The workshop instructor nailed it. I do identify with and champion the underdog in daily life and in my writing. Plus, I want to share my love of story and music with the world, in daily life and in my writing.

In my top favorite movie, *You've Got Mail*, the main character owns a bookshop that was passed down to her from her mother. The name of the bookshop is *Shop Around the Corner*.

I learned that the premise for this movie was based on two previous films. The first, by the same name, *Shop Around the Corner*, starring Jimmy Stewart, was about a leather goods shop instead of a bookshop. The second, retitled, *In the Good Old Summertime*, was the same plot made into a musical starring Judy Garland. It had a music shop instead of a bookshop. All three were about pen pals (or email pals in the case of my favorite film) who know each other but are antagonistic toward each other before they finally realize they have fallen in love.

The problem for Kathleen Kelly, the sweet bookshop owner in *You've Got Mail*, is that the big bad chain bookstore (Fox Books) has built a store right around the corner from hers. One day, while still fighting to keep her bookshop open—but realizing she is fighting a losing battle—Kathleen walked over to the children's department in Fox Books. While she sat there and looked around, she overheard a mother ask the clerk about a book a friend had recommended for her daughter to read. All the mother knew was *The Shoe Books*. The clerk had no idea. Kathleen wiped a tear from her eye and told him it was *The Shoe Books* by Noah Streatfield. The clerk asked her to spell the last name. She did, and she offered a suggestion as to which of the books to buy first. Dumbfounded, the clerk went to look for the title. The mother was grateful.

Unknown to Kathleen, Joe Fox overheard the entire conversation. He found out that day the difference between most discount store clerks and a book-loving independent bookshop owner.

Eventually, in spite of Kathleen's heroic efforts to overcome, she had to close the lovely bookshop that her mother left her. I always cry during the scene when she turns off the lights for the last time, flips the Open sign to Closed, and turns around to gaze at the empty shelves and tables. A smile appears on her face as she remembers her mother twirling her around in the space that was used for the Storybook Lady to share her books every week. The images fade, and Kathleen turns back toward the street, closes the door, and walks away. The camera focuses on a new sign on the door:

After 42 years we are closing our doors.
We have loved being part of your lives.

I am teary-eyed just writing about it!

The main character is the underdog, no doubt. But she had something the big store owner didn't have. He was a businessman who owned a bookstore. She was the Story Lady who shared her love of books with children every day.

I remember leaving the library for the last time after twelve years of working there. The bookshop owner in my favorite movie, after a heart-breaking loss, became a children's writer and loved her new-found purpose. I also found a new calling. Library director was a job I enjoyed more than any other, and I had a lot of jobs before I found that one! But I retired early in 2001, because my next assignment was to take care of my mother full-time, which allowed me to begin my writing career. I believe my parents, both in Heaven now for many years, know and are thrilled that I have become a writer. I can see them running down the streets of gold telling people to check out my books from the Heavenly Library!

"Now we know that all things work together for good for those who love God, who are called according to His purpose. Romans 8:28 TLV"

I love God's promises.

The other movies on my list also had many things to say to me, but this one resonated the most in my heart.

I think I'll watch it again.

What does my favorite movie have to do with my Kingdom Corner? Since my writing identity is centered around helping people (the underdogs) and sharing stories and music, my Kingdom Corner reminds me of that purpose. I surround myself with Scriptures, music CDs, photos of family and friends, inspirational quotes, a vision board, one or two collectibles, and at least a dozen books. (My space is limited in my camper.)

The point is, create your Kingdom Corner to be a place that you will love as much as Kathleen Kelly loved the bookshop her mother gave her. But switch it up sometimes. Doors open and close and dreams change and grow. So can Kingdom Corners. Wherever it is and however you decorate it, the Holy Spirit will be waiting for you when you arrive in your Kingdom Corner.

I still have dreams and visions for the future as far as my writing is concerned. I always wanted to own a bookshop like Shop Around the Corner. But in our technological world today, independent bookshops, and brick and mortar bookstores alike continue to have a hard time existing beside the many popular online book outlets.

So, the Lord gave me a new dream that relates to my original dream. My next book probably begins where the last one ended, though it will go a different direction and won't be a children's story. It will be about an underdog children's author who renovates an old train depot and establishes a magical bookshop filled with powerful stories to share and, in the corner, a stage for live music.

I've also begun collecting train memorabilia. Stay tuned.

Chapter Eight

◆

He's In Your Corner

Though the *Karate Kid* is one of my favorite movie trilogies, I am not a fan of professional boxing or wrestling. I don't think I have ever watched a fight on television, at least not through all the rounds to the final bell. I have never watched this type of sport in person, except in high school when a few cheerleaders were required to attend the wrestling matches. I did not enjoy that duty.

Before retirement and finding our property in the mountains, our camper was parked at a campground in Tennessee. After Dennis left school every Friday, we drove three hours to spend our weekends in the mountains, and then back to Hickory after church on Sunday morning. The next Friday we would escape the city again. One weekend, on the outskirts of Gatlinburg, Tennessee, we stopped by an artist's retail shop in a strip mall. Steven Sawyer's paintings are meticulously detailed and many include portraits of Jesus. You can see Sawyer's work at Art4God.com.

The print I came away with and put up on my Kingdom Corner wall is titled, "The Living Word." It is a painting of a young blonde girl sitting in a chair reading a book. In the background, standing waist-deep in a stream, Jesus leads the girl into the water to be baptized. Though you can't tell from the painting that the book is the Bible and the girl is reading about baptism, the title depicts it so. I own many pictures of people reading, but the longer I gazed at this painting, the more my eyes drifted to the baptism scene. The Holy Spirit whispered in my heart that when we are reading the Bible, whatever the passage or verse, we are immersed in the powerful truths and stories the Word contains.

The tender and loving Savior in the first Sawyer painting was in contrast to the next one I noticed of Jesus standing in the corner of a boxing ring. He had on boxing gloves and royal purple trunks. The expression on his face in this painting is amazing. It shows strength, power, and determination. The caption reads, "Undefeated." It immediately reminded me of "Champion of Love", the Gospel song written by Phil Cross and his wife and performed by the Cathedral Quartet. Jesus is our Undefeated Champion.

I researched the job description for a boxing manager/trainer and found that he sets up matches, supervises training, negotiates payments, and promotes his boxer to ensure a high turnout at matches. He wants the boxer to be as financially profitable as possible because he (the manager/trainer) receives a percentage of the profits. A good manager would never schedule a match without properly preparing his boxer for the specific competition he will face. The boxer must depend on his manager/trainer to handle his money, image, and career.

I also learned that the manager/trainer (or a coach or teammate he hires) is called the "corner-man." This individual stays out of the ring, but remains close by. He assists and instructs the fighter during the entire length of the bout. The instruction takes place between rounds. The cornerman is also responsible for giving minor medical aid, such as binding wounds and applying ice to stop bleeding and reduce swelling. He may also have to "throw in the towel" if the boxer is losing and could be injured permanently by continuing to fight.

After reading about the job of the cornerman in boxing, I discovered that there is also a cornerman in basketball. I happen to have an in-house expert on basketball in the person of my husband Dennis. He was a coach for 38 years and, since his retirement from the school system, he acts a basketball referee. I asked him what the term meant. He had never heard it before! He assumed it was someone who could hit a shot from the corner a large percentage of the time! Made sense to me, but to check a second source, I went to an online dictionary. It said that a good cornerman in basketball is a player who is talented and versatile enough, (and the right height) to play more than one position. On a five-man basketball team, a good cornerman can play point guard, forward, or center. I figure that would be as useful as guaranteed points shot from the corner of the floor.

After researching both these secular aspects of the term cornerman, I took some Kingdom Corner time to meditate and pray. What did the Bible have to say about corners? I found the verse that is at the beginning of this section. The Message Bible helped me apply the Word to my question and understand what Jeremiah 23:23-24 says:

"Am I not a God near at hand and not a God far off? Can anyone hide out in a corner where I can't see him? Am I not present everywhere, whether seen or unseen?"

Pondering all the aspects of the job of a boxing manager/trainer/cornerman, I saw a clear parallel to Jesus Christ. I concluded from both the written Word and what the Holy Spirit showed me from Scripture and other sources, that there is not a corner in this world where I am hidden from God. Sometimes I may want to run away from Him, or blame Him for my situation, but there's no use wasting the time and effort. He knows exactly where I am and how I got here. He knows what I'm thinking and feeling, whether it's the truth or a lie the devil has fooled me into believing.

The summer after my dad moved to Heaven, Dennis, Stacie, Mom, and I decided to go ahead and take the trip to the east coast that my dad had planned for us. We had several interesting times on that trip, but one sticks out to this day. We wanted to take a cruise on the Hudson River to see the New York City skyline at sunset. We were staying in New Jersey, and took a taxi across the river to the subway tunnel where we boarded a train that would take us to where the cruise line loaded. The tunnel was dirty and had a few people sitting by cardboard boxes, but we were looking forward to our cruise and didn't let it bother us too much. We had a wonderful cruise, and I am happy that we took a few beautiful photos of the Twin Towers that evening.

When the cruise was over, we stepped off the boat into the parking lot. We'd been told that a bus would be there to pick us up and take us back across the Washington Street Bridge to our hotel. There was no bus heading to New Jersey. A bus driver suggested we walk to the Port Authority and try to catch a bus there. It was several blocks away and by this time it was dark.

We walked, linked arm-in-arm, passing people on the sidewalk who stared at us as we walked by. I was so frightened in that moment, it was hard to move or even breathe, let alone hear God's Voice inside my heart telling me it would be all right. I wanted to be strong for Stacie, and thank God I wasn't alone. I had my mama and my husband with me!

We finally arrived at the Port Authority and stood there looking around. We didn't know where to go or who to ask for help. It definitely felt like we were stuck in a corner! As I looked around the huge room, I thought we were totally lost and there was no way to go back and find our way again. While we stood by the door looking like the midwest tourists we were, an officer came over and asked what in the world we were doing there. Mom told him our dilemma. He shook his head, pointed his finger, and firmly informed us that we needed to take the subway across the street and get out of there immediately! We asked no questions; we just obeyed.

The subway was a lot scarier in the dark. We discovered later that it was the subway train that took us into a bad neighborhood. It was the same one we had left from several hours earlier in the bright sunlight, excited to begin our adventure in New York City. We had backed ourselves into that corner by our own desire to go on a cruise in a place we weren't familiar with at all. We found ourselves all alone in the dark, not knowing what to do.

By the grace of God, we made it to the end of the subway line and found our original taxi stand where a very nice taxi-driver took us back across the river to our motel. We immediately booked him for the entire next day and a guided tour of the city!

The truth is that God was right there with us the entire evening. My God always goes before me and behind me, to my left and my right, is above me and below me. I'm surrounded by His love.

As an illustration of God's protection, I think of my friend Barri who is a Jewish believer. I shared in Stacie's book about how we met. Barri takes people to Israel twice yearly on mission trips through the organization, Sar Shalom Israel. These pilgrims, as she calls her teams, go and tell the people of the land about the Messiah. But they also bring tangible help to Holocaust survivors and patients in hospitals; clothes, blankets and quilts, stuffed animals and toys for the children. It is a wonderful organization to be part of and I am so very grateful to Barri for doing her assignment from God so I can be a part her mission trips through financially supporting her efforts.

Before one trip to Israel, I asked Barri to buy a Star of David necklace for me while she was there. She picked out a gorgeous one, sterling silver with a double-sided Star of shiny blue stones on one side and opalescent stones on the other. Soon after she gave it to me, I heard the story of the Star of David. The six sides of the Star mean that God goes before us, behind us, He's to our left, to our right, above us and beneath. Praise the LORD!

Not only is Jesus our Undefeated Champion, but when we are in the boxing ring of life and the devil is our ever-present opponent, Jesus is always in our corner. He is our Cornerman. He sets up divine connections for us, trains us in His Word and by His Spirit, and provides finances for living and giving. He wants us to succeed, and *not* because His percentage of the profits is 10%! God doesn't need our tithe or offerings. He paves His streets with gold! But our giving back to Him keeps the channel of BLESSING flowing between us. Like a good manager, God continues to set us up with opportunities that will bring more provision, so we can turn around and give back into the Kingdom. As a boxer must trust his manager and cornerman with his money, image, and career, we must trust our Champion/Cornerman to have our best interests at heart. As the boxing cornerman stays out of the ring but is nearby, God stays close to us. But as the boxer is expected to use his training, God also gives us free choice to use the training and tools He's provided in His Word. A boxer may get medical attention from his cornerman, but Jesus heals us everywhere we hurt.

In the same way the cornerman assists and instructs the fighter between rounds, my Cornerman whispers instructions to my heart during daily study and resting times in my Kingdom Corner. Sometimes it's necessary for a boxer's cornerman to "throw in the towel" because his fighter is losing and could be injured permanently if he continues to fight. That doesn't mean he's given up on the boxer. It means that he doesn't want him to die. He wants him to live to fight another day. In 1 Corinthians 10:13 we are told He has also provided a way of escape should we need one. In Joshua 10:11-13, the Lord was Joshua's Cornerman in subduing the Amorites when Joshua commanded the sun to stand still until the battle was won. In Deuteronomy 31:6, NKJV, we have this promise: *"Be strong and of good courage, do not fear nor be afraid of them; for the Lord your God, He is the One who goes with you. He will not leave you nor forsake you."*

We may call on Him to pull us out of a deadly situation the devil has gotten us into, but if we are so beaten up that we can't see the danger we are in, our Cornerman may "throw in the towel" and end the battle. The difference is that Jesus will wrap the towel around the devils' ankles and make him fall at ours!

I also realized that all these parallels speak to my calling as a writer. My Father is my publisher, taking His Word and giving it to me to give to people. The Holy Spirit is my editor, to assist me in the writing process, making sure every word is what He wants it to be. And the best news to me is that Jesus is my agent! He promotes me and my writing by providing divine connections to the people He had waiting to help my career, and the readers He wanted to touch through me.

The ultimate "towel thrown in the ring to save" was when Jesus tossed aside the graveclothes and the stone was rolled away. He went through great suffering in our place. No human cornerman would jump in the ring and fight the rest of the match for his injured boxer. But our divine Cornerman did just that. He left his Heavenly Home, came to earth, lived, died, and rose triumphant from the grave for you and me. He fought yesterday, so we could win forever.

This is not the first time, and won't be the last, that time spent in my Kingdom Corner with the Word of God and the Holy Spirit is what allowed me to discover a connection between something I would never have thought on my own (the sport of boxing) and *our all-time, undisputed, undefeated, Champion of Love.*

Every time that happens is a wonder to me. And I know if I will give Him a little bit more of my time every day in my Kingdom Corner, many more wonders await.

Chapter Nine

◆

The Corner Market

There is continual debate about when a human's memories begin. I know one person who thinks he remembers coming through the birth canal into the waiting doctor's hands! I have my reservations about that. But most people have vague memories of being a toddler, maybe as young as two or three.

My mother documented that I took my first steps at nine months. So I could have been quite young in my first memories of climbing around our three-story home. I remember my little "art studio" under the basement stairs. In that marvelous nook, despite the bugs that came out to terrorize me periodically, I was free to splash paint or draw with crayons on the work table Mom built for my brother and me to develop our artistic side.

I also remember standing, closely supervised, on a stool in front of our kitchen stove. One of the first things Mom taught me to cook was pudding. Well, she taught me how to stir the pudding mix until it boiled. Even that is almost a lost art. Today people usually want things to happen as fast as possible. But I enjoy taking it slow. I still use "Cook and Serve" pudding instead of instant.

I cringe at memories of our second-story bedrooms with no air-conditioning. It makes me sweat just thinking about them! But the sleeping porch at the end of the hall provided cooler nights of rest in the hot Kansas summer. In cooler weather we used the attic for play. There, among the Christmas decorations and old furniture, adventures were around every corner. An old mattress provided a nice tumbling mat, though I never was good at tumbling. From the beginning, gymnastics was not my calling. I mastered the forward roll, or somersault, but that was about it. I was the only cheerleader on our squad who could not do a cartwheel! I loved the eerie atmosphere and musty smell of the attic in a rainstorm. That memory made it into a book.

My first memories of venturing outside beyond the confines of our yard happened when several times a week, Mom put me into a stroller, or later took me by the hand, and we walked a block and a half to the corner market. This grocery store was a place of wonder for me for several reasons. First, it was owned by two sets of twins. In the 1950's, the twin Murray brothers, Bob and Al, married twin sisters, Vera and Verna. They opened Murray's Market. I never could tell them apart unless they were in the place in the market where they usually worked. But back then, it didn't matter if I knew their first names. All four of them were Mr. or Mrs. Murray.

The second thing I loved about Murray's Market was that in the first aisle stood a *huge*, to my child's eyes, stainless steel coffee pot. Tiny cups waited, stacked by the real sugar dispenser and a carton of creamer. Mom never missed the opportunity to sip a cup of coffee while shopping. She started me out on the habit very early. Granted, my cup was about a third cup of coffee. The rest was cream, with several shakes of sugar tossed in. Even after stirring, when I drained the liquid, I enjoyed slurping up the wet sugar that had accumulated at the bottom of the cup. Though I now drink it black or with a little cream, I guess the corner market is the place I learned to like coffee. It's Mom's fault.

The employees at Murray's Market all knew Mom, and she knew them by name. She ordered canned goods by the case, and when a shipment came in we were allowed to walk up the steep ramp into the back storage room. Stacked-up boxes of groceries surrounded us as we made arrangements with Claude, the produce man, to have our order on the pick-up ramp when we were done shopping. We usually walked to the store, but on order pick-up days we drove the car.

My favorite thing about the Murray's corner market came about when my brother David and I were probably about five and three. Mom allowed us to walk together to the store to buy small amounts of groceries. David had one certain privilege first, since he's eighteen months older than I am. I watched in awe, and with a bit of jealousy, as Vera or Verna rang up our groceries, and wrote the total on a little pad. She'd hand it to my brother and in his very nice left-handed writing, he signed his name. The carbon copy was torn off, added to our loaded sack, and we walked back home.

Finally the day came when I was five or six, and Mom decided I was old enough to run to the store all by myself. Times were very different then. Parents weren't afraid to let their children out to play or run short errands on foot. Every house on the block had a parent watching out for all the kids in the neighborhood. Mom arranged with the neighbor across the alley for me to cut through her backyard. That way I wouldn't be out on the street without somebody watching me. Edna was our hairdresser, and always waved at me from the window by her hair-cutting chair. She had a clear view to the store parking lot. I think Mom called her every time I left the house, so one of them could keep an eye on me the whole trip. Not only could I walk by myself, but I had earned the same right my brother had. I had Mom's authority to say, "Charge it, please," and sign my name to Vera or Verna's little pad!

My signature, even printed and not cursive, carried the same authority as Mom signing the charge slip. The name signed was a promise to the Murrays that Mom would pay the bill at the end of the month. That way of doing business with a corner market is unheard of today, but I will never forget that grown-up feeling of charging our supper. I had the power! The entire grocery store was at my fingertips! Now, if I veered from the list Mom gave me too often, that wasn't a good thing either! I imagine I was given permission to add a candy bar in there once in a while.

In the same way, God's children have the power of the Name of Jesus to obtain whatever we need. Learning to use that powerful Name is something that I spend much time reading, studying, and praying about in my Kingdom Corner. Over the years I have realized that it is there, in my secret place with the Holy Spirit that I need to learn how and when to use His Name. Then I practice using it in my prayers for people and situations in my life where the power of the Name of Jesus may be the only thing that can change things.

The reason I used my name when I signed those charge slips at Murray's was that Mom wanted to know if it was my brother or me buying the groceries. But if I had had her permission and she had let the Murrays know it, I could have signed her name. Jesus not only gave me permission to use His Name, He *wants* me to use it! Another wonderful thing about the power of His Name is that though the signed charge slip was Mom's promise to pay the corner market later, Jesus has already paid the price for us on Calvary. When we use His Name we have the assurance that whatever we ask for has already been purchased by His sacrifice on the cross!

Because I belong to Him, I have the authority to use His Name and get the same results He would. But I have to know what the Word says about me as a believer, and how to make those promises mine now. That process takes Kingdom Corner time first. I need time spent in the Word to learn what belongs to me. I then use my prayer time to practice what He has taught me, by listening to the Holy Spirit and praying through Him in the Name of Jesus. The next step is to go out into the world and do what He has called me to do. As one of my mother's favorite songs says, "His Name is Wonderful."

One of the most powerful things about the Name of Jesus is learning how to use it to beat up on the devil and keep him out of our lives. The last home Dennis and I lived in before retirement had originally had a crawl-space foundation. A previous owner remodeled and added a back deck. To support the deck and create an open storage area underneath, he dug into the ground and cleared enough dirt under the deck to get even with the outside back wall. Then he continued to dig under the house all the way to the front. This created a dugout dirt basement that went all the way under the house and joined the original crawl space underneath the front porch.

Though we had to unlock the door at the back to gain entry, the front part of our dirt basement was open to the elements and to all kinds of little creatures like mice, squirrels, spiders, and crickets. Many found nice homes in our boxes before I discovered that cardboard corroded and fell apart quickly in the humidity. I had to exchange boxes with plastic bins and tight lids. I had a lot of boxes of stuff from our previous home, but there wasn't room to unpack them in the smaller house. After securing everything in bins, we covered the dirt and sand floor with plastic and set the bins on top. I was glad we had the extra storage space for the newly repacked household goods and the storage area to hold tools, the furnace, and water heater, and to give easier access to the under-workings of the house.

It was a nasty basement, though, and I avoided it as much as possible! When our water heater went out, we had to replace it. The plumber came, and he made a scary discovery in our dirt basement. When he pulled out the old water heater, he found, not one but TWO, snake skins curled around the pipes behind it! I shuddered when I saw them. Thank the Lord I never saw one single live snake in the nine years we lived there. But here was proof that they had slithered in.

The door had been closed and locked, but the snakes sneaked in through the cracks in the foundation and the area that was left open in the front. I rarely thought about the possibility and did nothing to make the basement airtight. Perhaps because we knew we weren't going to be there forever, we chose to ignore what could happen and live with it the way it was. The ol' serpent invaded our house because we hadn't taken the time to seal it shut.

The devil knows his time is short and he's going to do everything he can to creep into our lives through any crack we leave open. He uses strife, sickness, depression, confusion, lack, even being too busy, and every other evil thing, to stick his foot in the cracks and damage our lives. The best way to keep those cracks sealed, begins with time spent with God in our Kingdom Corners.

As a little girl, Murray's Market was the place I learned the power and authority of using the right name. I believe there's not much time left for us to make our lives here on earth count for the Kingdom. We need to spend time with God, no matter when or where we choose to do so. We must learn how to use the Name of Jesus to bring more people into the Kingdom and accomplish our individual Kingdom assignments.

Time is short. Jesus is coming soon, my friend. In fact, I believe the day of His return is right around the corner.

Chapter Ten

◆

Brighten the Corner
Where You Are

I began singing Southern Gospel music when I was twenty-four years old. In 1978, during his first year of teaching, Dennis took over as tenor and piano player for the Messengers Quartet from Silver Lake, Kansas. Two years later, their baritone singer left. Because I have a low voice range and knew the songs, I was asked to fill in until they found a new singer. That temporary position lasted for the next twenty-two years! We ministered all over the nation's heartland, singing two or more concerts every weekend. We had the honor to open for many big name Gospel groups.

One of my first quartet singing experiences was at the yearly concert the Messengers had with the Blackwood Brothers Quartet. I remember standing beside James Blackwood in his pristine white suit. I was star-struck and VERY nervous to sing in front of Mr. Gospel Music! It was the first of many concerts where we were privileged to sing on the same stage with such legendary artists as J.D. Sumner (who sang backup for Elvis with his Stamps Quartet), Jake Hess (who sang lead for the Statesmen Quartet and later formed the original Imperials), and one of my favorite female singers, Lilly Fern

Weatherford, whose tenor voice blended perfectly with a male quartet. She was an inspiration to me and I aspired to blend with the guys like she did!

I can't recall when I first heard the song, Brighten the Corner Where You Are, but I know I have heard many different groups perform it. I found several recordings of it on YouTube, two of which were performed by the Blackwood Brothers and the Statesmen. When I looked up the lyrics and story behind the song, I found that the writer was a woman named Ina Mae Duley Ogdon, who wrote the original poem with that title. As a woman preaching the Gospel in the 1860's, she pioneered women in the pulpit. But Ina Mae had to put her dream of preaching and ministry on hold to care for her sick elderly father. She experienced anger and resentment at first, but she overcame those emotions and expressed how she did so by writing the poem. The words encouraged others to serve the Lord in whatever ways and circumstances they find themselves. The poem featured the Scripture found in Matthew 5:14-16:

"Ye are the Light of the world. A city that is set on a hill cannot be hidden. Neither do men light a candle and put it under a bushel, but on a candle stick; and it giveth light unto all that are in the house. Let your light so shine before men, that they may see your good works, and glorify your Father which is in Heaven."

The third and fourth stanzas are ones we don't always hear recorded by singers. They are my favorite verses. They talk about the talents we have been given, and how surely someone in the world needs what we have to offer. The words also remind us that Jesus is the Bright and Morning Star, and we reflect Him when we feed others the Bread of Life. As believers, we possess the very thing that the world needs most, our Savior and Lord, Jesus Christ. He alone holds the love, restoration, and comfort they need.

The fifth stanza sums it up and directly relates to my message in *Kingdom Corner Connection.* "Stay in fellowship with Jesus and behold His face, if His glorious radiance you'd impart." In other words, spend time with God first, then go out and serve others. No matter where we find ourselves or what circumstances we are in, if we use our God-given talents to spread His love and life, we will touch people's hearts and "brighten the corner where we are."

My Kingdom Corner holds a very special table lamp. It lights my Bible so I can read it, brightens my writing space, and warms my heart with the memory of the way it came to me. The lamp was my last Mother's Day gift from my precious daughter. I will never forget the day that we both spied the lamp sitting in the back of a booth at *Fantastic Finds*, one of our favorite antique malls in Hickory, North Carolina. Stacie and I treasured our mother-daughter days, and spent many of them antiquing. From the time she was a little girl, we enjoyed hunting for antique treasures. It was "our thing." I am so grateful for those special days and the sweet memories they give me.

On the day we saw the lamp, Stacie was at the end of her chemo treatments and sported one of her many hats. She kept teaching the entire time she was in treatment, usually only taking the day after chemo off in order to recuperate. My girl loved her "kids," and most of her students knew what was going on with "Miss Stacie" and why she didn't have any hair. She loved wearing hats for them, and they expected her to have on a different hat every day of the week! She probably had enough to last two or three weeks.

I will never forget how Stacie looked at me that day, clutching the lamp and smiling. Oh, that girl's smile! Stacie grabbed the lamp before I barely got a good look at it and said, "Mom, you need this. Happy Mother's Day!"

She went Home to Heaven a few weeks later, on Father's Day. Later we discovered the Father's Day gift she had bought early for Dennis. Through our tears we could both "see" her smiling face and her look that said, "Surprise!" That's our Stacie. She may have been backed into some rough and scary corners, but she brightened every place she went with the light of her smile and her heart.

The lamp Stacie bought for me that day has a ceramic base with two adorable rabbits in a comfy chair reading a book together. The shade is a quilted pattern in navy and burgundy plaid. That lamp will always grace my Kingdom Corner. Stacie was right. I needed it.

I have always liked blue lights. Blue lights on the dashboard of my vehicles was always a plus when deciding on which car to buy. Blue lights on sound equipment, clocks, or anything with light-up dials or numbers are my first purchase choice. While most people enjoy bright red, green, white, or multi-colored lights at Christmas, my tree and house are decorated with blue twinkle lights and decor.

So when it came time to write a story where I needed to "show" the Holy Spirit character was present, I chose to encase Him in a sparkly blue shaft of light. The blue light showed up whenever Gahlay Rahzeen, the Revealer of Mysteries, was called upon. Sometimes He came to the character's Kingdom Corner at home, but it didn't matter where the characters were or how many called on Him at the same moment. When they called, the glittering blue light showed up.

In the same way, the Holy Spirit comes to us wherever we are. Blue light or not, He is the essence of brightening the corner where we are! It doesn't matter if we are in our usual Kingdom Corner or outside in our favorite quiet spot, on a mountain, on the beach, or where we work. He is there with us and anywhere we meet with Him becomes our Kingdom Corner. As believers, the Holy Spirit lives inside us. We take Him wherever we go. That fact bears thinking about.

We are the ones who bring His light to others. Like the song says, we "brighten the corner where we are" by taking the light within us and sharing it with the world. We do this by using whatever talents and gifts God has given us. Some of us write books, others write and sing songs. Some paint pictures, take photographs, preach, or are in full-time ministry. Some play professional sports. The creative and performing arts, as well as being in ministry, are sometimes referred to as our calling or our natural bent. These can be the most visible talents and gifts.

God has also called teachers, caregivers, farmers, volunteers, doctors, nurses, lawyers, accountants, bankers, cooks, seamstresses, construction workers, electricians, plumbers, or any other service job. Whatever your Kingdom assignment is, it requires skills and talents whether gained from education, hard work to develop what is needed to do the job, or supernaturally given by the grace of God. Our amazing Father has equipped His children with whatever is needed to help others. His ultimate purpose is to bring everybody into the family. I Peter 3:9 says that God desires all to come to repentance. Every person must choose to do so or not. God uses each and every one of His children to accomplish this task and to help others make the choice to come to Him. We are His hands in this world. We are the "light that shines before men, that they may see our good works, and glorify your Father which is in Heaven." (Matthew 5:16.)

The cover of this book came about because of a dear friend I met in high school. Bob was my sophomore biology partner and the only reason I passed the course. We became good friends and discussed spiritual things often. While I was a cheerleader, I supported him by attending many of his cross country races. I still have the winning number he wore from the day he set the school record. When we were juniors, I invited him to attend a Campus Life Youth for Christ meeting with me. It was shortly after that night that he was persuaded to make the choice to follow Jesus.

When I married Dennis and Bob married Diane, we moved many miles apart, but still kept in touch by mail and email. Over the years, we enjoyed several visits with Bob and Diane. They both enjoyed antiquing too, so that was a common interest. Bob retired as a Vice-President from Pioneer Hi-Bred, (an agricultural seed business), and soon after that his wonderful wife went Home to Heaven after a long fight with breast cancer. Because Stacie was already in Heaven at the time, we forged a new bond. I shared with him that Diane and Stacie probably got together to browse the Golden Street Antique Shops and laugh about our biology days! Bob is kind of a serious guy, but I think he liked that idea.

Bob is now an assistant pastor, and Dennis and I had the honor of attending a service in 2019 where he preached. I felt like a proud mom! In a way, I guess I am his spiritual mother (even though he is older than I am.) Bob told about the night I took him to Campus Life and he soon after accepted the Lord.

When I needed a cover for his book, I remembered that Bob's cousin Mark is a photographer. Bob had sent me two photos that Mark had taken of the Smoky Mountains. I was impressed. When I looked at Mark's website, I saw several photos of the Northern Lights taken in the Grand Tetons of Canada. I emailed him, reminded him of my friendship with Bob, and told him about the "Blue Light" of the Holy Spirit character in my *Tresia* series. I asked if he would be willing to photoshop the Northern Lights photo to accommodate my shining blue shaft theme. He agreed, and you hold in your hand the beautiful result.

I led Bob to Jesus in high school, and all these years later, he led me to his cousin. Mark provided what I needed now; a gorgeous book cover that shows my readers that there is a shining light called the Holy Spirit Who is listening and will come brighten the corner where they are.

All you have to do is enter your Kingdom Corner and call on Him.

PART II
The Corner

———————◆———————

Connect Points

Chapter Six: In My Own Little Corner

Do you have a special place or places where you meet with God on a daily basis? If so, write about it, or tell a friend why you chose it.

If not, make a list of tangible things you would include if you make one: (special chair, bookshelf, photos, wall décor, mementos, etc.)

What kind of atmosphere would you like to create? What colors, music, candles, or scents would you use to create that atmosphere?

If you want to, create or redesign your individual Kingdom Corner and share it with a friend or family member, or me! You could also do this as a group project with friends and share photos or visit each other's Kingdom Corners.

Do you choose a Word of the Year? If not, do you like the idea? Ask God to show you what word to choose. Find a verse of Scripture that relates to your word. Since I began this focus, my Words of the Year and corresponding verses are:

- 2012 – Chosen – Psalm 119:30
- 2013 – Plans – Jeremiah 29:11
- 2014 – Glory – II Corinthians 3:18
- 2015 – Restoration – Psalm 23:3

- 2016 – Increase – II Corinthians 9: 8-11 AMPC
- 2017 – Prepare – Psalm 5:3
- 2018 – Deeper – Colossians 1: 9-10
- 2019 – Practice – Joshua 1:8
- 2020 – Rebuild – Isaiah 54: 11-12

In 2016, I began to create a yearly vision board, thanks to another young Bible teacher who inspired this sixty-something woman to do so. Terri Savelle Foy has a wonderful book, *Dream It, Pin It, Live It*, and an online course about making and using a vision board (www.terri.com). That is where I put up my Word of the Year and illustrate my goals for the year and beyond. (It really does make a difference to keep things in front of your eyes.) I base my yearly goals, written down in a Terri Savelle Foy *My Personal Dreams and Goals* notebook, to my Word of the Year whenever it applies. What creative ways can you remind yourself of your word and how to apply it? How do or could you use a prayer journal?

Prayer is a priority in my Kingdom Corner time. I use a prayer journal to write down special requests and the names of those I pray for regularly. I list specific names or groups for each weekday. I begin with praise and thanksgiving, then I pray for our leaders (I Timothy 2:1-3) and the people in my prayer journal. Last, I pray about any personal concerns or needs.

Chapter II: Shop Around the Corner

Write down your top 3-5 movies, TV shows, and/or books. Do they have a common thread? Do your favorites tell you anything about your identity as it relates to your Kingdom assignment? (Like mine is writing.)

If you like this idea, ask the Lord if He has a special name He calls you. Is there a story from your life behind the answer you hear from Him? Journal about the name you heard, and/or share the story with a friend.

Do you have a special name, or what name would you choose for God, and why? In my *Tresia* series, I use different words for the Three in One. They are Ahvee, which means my Father, Hah D'Var, which means the Word, and Gahlay Rahzeen, the Revealer of Mysteries. I often use these names in my prayers because they are special to me. Do you have three separate names for your conversations in prayer with the three Persons of the Trinity? If not, think about or journal what those names would be. I used the Hebrew words for my characters' names, but they could come from scriptures also.

Do you have a dream that hasn't happened yet, but you still want to come true in your life? Journal about it or make a vision board and share it with a friend. Have a Vision Board party! Dream BIG!

Chapter Eight: He's In Your Corner

I had never thought about how boxing relates to the Christian walk or my Kingdom assignment. Is there a subject on which you have received new revelation after asking the Lord about it? Journal and/or share with a friend.

Practice asking for specific answers to questions you have, or a subject or question you want more light on. Write those things down and use your Kingdom Corner time to seek answers from the Word and from the Holy Spirit. Journal and/or share about your experience.

Check out Sar Shalom Israel's website (www.sarshalomisrael.org), and ask the Lord if He would have you be involved in any way with this or a similar organization. If interested, study other Jewish traditions and their history, such as the mezuzah, menorah, Hanukkah, or the feasts and celebrations.

Do you have a favorite painting or song about Jesus that speaks to you? Write about it, and/or share with a friend.

Chapter Nine: The Corner Market

Discuss, think about, or journal the following:

What are your earliest memories? Is there a connection to any of your early memories and a Biblical passage or principal, such as my memory of the corner market and our authority to use the Name of Jesus?

Do you use the Name of Jesus? In what specific situation do you use His Name and why?

Do you remember a dark time in your life when the devil infiltrated your family? Was there anything you could have done earlier to keep him out? What steps can you take now to keep him out the next time he tries to hurt you or your family?

This chapter was about how Jesus gave us authority to use His Name and what a privilege and honor it is to do so. How do you think Jesus must feel when His Name is used in vain, as a curse word said in anger?

How do you think it makes Jesus feel to see and hear us use His name with the power and authority He intended us to have?

Chapter Ten: Brighten the Corner Where You Are

Had it not been for time spent with God in my Kingdom Corner, I would not have known when one season of my life ended and another was beginning. We sang Southern Gospel Music for over thirty years, with the quartet in Kansas, and then as a family in the Macs. Leaving Kansas was hard for us, but because I was seeking God in my Kingdom Corner time, we knew God was leading us to North Carolina and a family ministry. Most people didn't understand and even told us we were making a big mistake. In hindsight, we are so glad we had those nine years singing with our daughter. When Stacie moved to Heaven, that ministry and season naturally ended. But I still needed to spend time with God to know what He had next for us, especially after Dennis retired. Take some time to think about the changing seasons in your life. Do you see how God led you from one to the other? Did you fight His leading, or did you just trust and obey, even in spite of how it looked and other opinions? What made you finally decide it was time to leave one season and go on to another? Journal or share it.

Look up all the words to the song, Brighten the Corner Where You Are. Is there a certain stanza, or more than one, to which you especially relate? Why? Journal or share your answer.

What practical things can you do to brighten your corner in the world? Make a list and do them.

If the Holy Spirit is inside you and goes with you wherever you are, think about the things you're doing together. Is He glad or grieved at your activities? If you think He might be grieved, make a list of activities you need to stop doing.

I told you about the lamp in my Kingdom Corner and why it's special to me. I found this verse that helped me see the deeper meaning. Psalm 18:28 CEV says, *"Lord, you give light to my lamp. My God brightens the darkness around me."* Can you pick out a certain object that brightens your life? Can you find a scripture that relates? Look for it and write it down.

Do you have a friend or family member, who you spent time with in your younger days, and with whom you have stayed in touch, in spite of distance and life in general? Think about why that is. What first drew you to each other and still connects you with that person? Has something impacted your life recently in connection with them? If they are still around, take time to call, write, or visit them soon and tell them how they have brightened your life.

"Write down the things you read, learn, and hear while you meet with Us in your Kingdom **Corner** *every day. Mysteries revealed, treasures discovered, hidden secrets opened."*

Gahlay Rahzeen, Revealer of Mysteries
Trinity Tales of Tresia, Book III,
A Perfectly Magnificent Cane

PART III

THE CONNECTION

Connec'tion, *noun*

The act of joining or state of being joined, knit, or linked together, as something *intervening or by weaving together.

* Interve'ning, *adjective*
Coming or being between persons, things, or points of time.

———————◆———————

*"In prayer there is a **connection** between what God does and what you do.*

You can't get forgiveness from God, for instance, without also forgiving others.

If you refuse to do your part, you cut yourself off from God's part."

Matthew 13:51-52 The Message (MSG)

Chapter Eleven

◆

Beginnings Connection

When the leaves start to turn colors, I begin to seek my next "Word of the Year." At the same time, I also ask the Lord what book, passage, or Bible subject He wants me to study that relates to that word. In 2020, my Bible study has centered around "Beginnings" in the book of Genesis, and the ministry of Jesus in the Gospels of John and Mark. My word for this year is "rebuild." God wanted me to go back to the beginning of my walk with Him and rebuild things that I had let slip over the past couple years, such as making my time with God my first priority instead of working Him into *my* schedule. I needed to go back to the basics, the foundations of my faith, and renew my soul and spirit by sitting at His feet and learning of Him. I also wanted to embrace new things He has for me, and to do so I had to commit to time every day in my Kingdom Corner.

As I thought about beginnings, my mind was drawn back to the beginning of my relationship with Dennis. We met in seventh and eighth grade, but we started dating when I was a senior and he was a junior in high school. It was quite a scandal when we became engaged after *my* graduation! Dennis went through his entire senior year engaged to me. We married two and a half months after his graduation in 1974, when we were both eighteen years old. In later years, as a school counselor, Dennis tried to steer clear of personal questions about the best age to get married! But in our case, because the Lord was in it from the beginning, it's worked out well. I'm sure many others have the same testimony. Sometimes it's good to grow up together.

A few months before the wedding, my mother happened to see a house for sale in a nice area, close to where I grew up. We looked at it together. Mom always thought rent was a waste of money. Equity in a home was the way to go. Before Dennis ever saw the house or even knew about it, we were at the bank and Mom co-signed a loan for me to buy that house. It was a good "beginner" house, but I still can't believe that I bought it without Dennis knowing. I remember showing it to him, only to say "Surprise! It's ours." I honestly don't remember his initial reaction, but because my husband is a very easy-going guy, we moved into the house immediately after the honeymoon and began our married life. Stacie was born in that little airplane bungalow. Though it is now in a terrible run-down neighborhood, it will always hold a special place in our hearts.

Five years later, we were ready to move east of Topeka so Den could be closer to the school where he taught. Mom stepped in again and bought that first house from us to use as a rental.

(My mom was a wheeler-dealer!) Mom and Dad had bought a little lake house south of town for a weekend getaway, but they decided to move there after Dad retired. So Dennis, Stacie, and I moved into the house where I had lived as a teenager. We "rented to own" the house my parents had built and vacated. In hindsight, we would have been much better off financially if we had bought the house from them at the great price they offered, but there was a problem. It was Mom's house, not mine. And she had a key.

Much to my parents' dismay, we decided to go into debt again and move to the west side of town, where we built "our" house. We were singing with the Messengers by then, and chose to build in a location that was close to where we met the quartet bus, thus giving us a short drive home on late weekend nights when we returned from a concert. Dennis chose to make the longer commute to school every weekday. That drive became his Kingdom Corner time, where God readied him to meet the new school day.

It worked out well for me, since I never would have landed my Silver Lake Library director job if we hadn't moved into the community. Dennis was established in his career, and distance from school didn't make that much difference other than drive time. Since the beginning of our marriage, though, I had worked at several jobs but had never had one that I enjoyed. Or if I did, the job didn't last. I finally found my niche at the library. It was a God thing. Although I had loved reading and libraries since I was a little girl, this job was the beginning of my connection to His plan for my life. The Silver Lake Library was where my love for books could be used and where the first seeds of a desire to be an author were planted.

We lived for eighteen years in the berm home we built. With three sides of our house built into the ground, if there was a tornado warning, we never had to worry about going to the basement. We lived in one. It was also easy to have my quiet time with God on the roof of my house. The back roofline was a foot off the ground. We designed that house, and it was our dream home for that time. I was surprised that I wasn't brokenhearted when we decided to sell it. Stacie had already moved to North Carolina, Dad had gone Home to Heaven, and Mom needed me. We sold that house, I "retired" after twelve years at the library, and we moved into the lake house with Mom so I could be her full-time caregiver. She was dealing with health issues by then and I wanted to be close by. We knew the Lord was calling us to North Carolina, so that seemed the best move while we waited for God's timing to begin a new season.

Looking back at our houses in Kansas, I see so many connections. The first house connected us to Den's college days and Stacie's birth. The second house connected us to Mom and Dad providing us with a better financial stability for a time, and a much nicer house than we could have otherwise afforded. The third house that we built connected us to our singing ministry and my library job. The last house we lived in connected me to Mom and allowed me to be what she needed in her senior years.

Now that we have lived in four different places in North Carolina, I see how the connections have continued. Our first North Carolina realtor connected us with our home in Morganton, even though it was a "For Sale by Owner" that we happened to drive by while looking at his listings. It was pretty much our dream cabin and by buying it, we were able to bless a couple who were going into full-time ministry and needed to sell fast. Mom joined us after six months, and we lived with three generations in that cabin. We had begun our family singing trio with Stacie by then, but she still lived two hours away and needed to be closer. She moved in with us while looking for a job. Stacie had her private space in the loft, and we built Mom a studio apartment in the back of the house.

When we left Kansas, Dennis decided to use his second Masters Degree. He switched from high school vocal music to a new counseling career at a nearby middle school only five minutes away from our new home in North Carolina. I was connected to my first writers group via my dear church friend Carol, who invited me to attend with her. Carol was a major connection for me. I adored her, and we became fast friends. I learned early on that being part of a vibrant and skilled writers critique group was an advantage many new writers don't have. I highly recommend finding a good one. But beware, not all writers groups are the same, so be diligent. Not having that weekly in-person connection with other writers was one of the hardest things about moving to the mountains. Thankfully, I still have wonderful friends (and online editors) from the Morganton Writers Group.

Mom went to Heaven in 2006, and my assignment as her caregiver ended. God gave me a special grace to take care of my mom for a season. I wouldn't trade those seven years I had with her, but I knew she was in Heaven with Jesus and Daddy. It's hard to grieve with that perspective. I missed her, but she left me a piece of her heart in her little dog J.J., who adopted me as his mama right away! A new season of pursuing my call to write began in earnest.

After a couple years of substitute teaching, Stacie went back to school to earn another degree. She switched from music just like her dad had done and received her Master's Degree in Exceptional Children. She moved out on her own with a wonderful new job as the EC Coordinator at New Dimensions Charter School (NDS) in Morganton.

After five years of middle school, Dennis decided to return to high school kids and coaching. He sent out his resume and only a few days passed before God connected him to a job tailor-made for him. The way it came about was definitely a God connection with a wonderful Christian principal.

Dennis was able to use both of his degrees, music and counseling, as well as his love for coaching basketball and tennis. But the drive time after practice and games back to Morganton got old fast. Besides the commute, our large dream cabin felt very empty with just the two of us. We decided to move to Hickory. Living eight minutes from his school was a blessing for the next nine years.

In 2011 our world changed drastically. Stacie was diagnosed with lymphoma and she moved back in with us while undergoing chemo treatments. When she wasn't able to drive herself, I would take her to school or we would meet a fellow teacher who drove through Hickory on her way to NDS. The first half of 2012 was long and hard. But we all learned how to have faith over fear. Stacie chose a saying for that time that we lived by through all the ups and downs. "God's Got This." Now Dennis and I wear bracelets with her name that say, "God's Still Got This." He has Stacie in Heaven, and He has us here on earth.

After a couple months, Dennis and I began to seek the Lord for a new beginning and our next connection. We explored many possibilities. Dennis applied to schools in Virginia, Kentucky, and Tennessee. We met some great people and visited a few good churches. In the end, though, we felt like God wanted him to stay at his school in Hickory until retirement.

After spending several years as "weekend campers" in Tennessee, something happened that was a major new beginning for us. We found our church in Cherokee, North Carolina. The amazing connection story about how we ended up there is documented in Stacie's book and the next chapter of this one. The result of this connection was that we knew God was leading us to the mountains of western North Carolina. With help from friends at church we moved our camper to a campground in Franklin and began to look for a house or land.

When Dennis retired, both our homes in Morganton and Hickory sold in record time. We were debt-free for the first time in our married life with only monthly campground and storage unit fees. It didn't take us long to find our new dream place. Dennis wanted to buy land and build another house. God had Macs MountainView waiting for us, and we knew it the minute we stepped onto the four acres in Cowee Valley. It took us a year of living at the campground before we were ready to move onto the property. Since moving to the mountains in the summer of 2018, many steps have already been taken toward our dream. We look forward to the fulfillment of the vision we have been given. God is still revealing all He wants us to do, but our new assignment includes writing, music, and hospitality. (Willingness to do that last part is a miracle for me. When I took a spiritual gifts test many years ago, hospitality was last on the list!)

God connections in our lives have been the norm from the beginning of our marriage. Every new beginning came about because of divine connections. I directly attribute both the connections and our finding and following them, to time spent with God in my Kingdom Corner. I may not have even realized at the time what those moments would produce, but God did. He had it all planned from the beginning of time.

The Old and New Testaments, or the First and Second Covenants as I like to call them, have revealed truths that I needed to consciously and deliberately rebuild into my life this year. They are truths I have known since I became of child of God at the age of eight, but I asked the Lord for new revelations concerning my connection to the Father, Son, and Holy Spirit.

As I began my study of Genesis this year, I reread the Creation account first. I used to struggle with how God created something that suddenly was without form and void. Wait a minute. Doesn't God do everything perfectly from the beginning? Yes, He does.

I believe that there is a space of time between Genesis 1:1 and Genesis 1:2, as much time as true science requires. Some call this the "Gap or Restoration Theory." It has its supporters and detractors, but it is the explanation that makes the most sense to me. Something catastrophic happened between these first two verses, and there is Scriptural evidence in Isaiah 14:13-14, that it was the fall of Lucifer from Heaven. Jesus told His disciples about it in Luke 10:18.

My short allegory based on the *Tresia* books, *A Glimpse*: *The Truly Excellent Scepter*, includes scenes that expound on my imagination's view of how Lucifer fell and what happened afterwards. The allegory is included at the beginning of Book III and is the connection between the second and third books. For me, and I hope my readers, this scenario fills in the gap between the end of Book II and the beginning of Book III, as well as the gap between the first "Beginning" in Genesis 1:1 and the second "Beginning" in Genesis 1:2. You may not agree with this conclusion, but study it out for yourself and ask the Lord if there is a connection.

The two Gospels I chose to study this year contain two different accounts of the life of Jesus. They start at different beginnings, John with Jesus as "the Word" at the beginning of the Genesis Creation, and Mark with the baptism of Jesus and the beginning of His ministry. With these two Second Covenant books, I am rebuilding my view of Jesus. He is the Word, God the Son, a man who came to save mankind, and my Savior and Lord.

The beginning connection between the Creator and His children is one that I have concentrated on this year in my Kingdom Corner time. This connection reminds me of the teaching in John 15. In nature, the branches are natural or grafted in. Both must stay connected to the vine if growth is to occur and fruit to appear. The Jews are God's chosen people, the natural branches, but as Christians, we've been adopted or grafted into the family of

God. We must continue to abide in Jesus, the true Vine, if we want to grow and develop the spiritual knowledge and power to accomplish our Kingdom assignments.

I have always loved this parable in the fifteenth chapter of John about our connection to the Father and Jesus. It takes me back to my childhood and the beginning of my relationship with God. Everything in my life since then has been connected to the time I spend with Him, even way before I called the place we meet, my "Kingdom Corner."

Friend, from this moment on, I urge you to make a new beginning. Nourish your God-connection by spending time together with your Father, Jesus, and the Holy Spirit. Greet God with praise and worship, feed on His Word, and in earnest prayer, seek His unique plan and assignment for you. That beginning will connect you not only with His plan for you right now, but also to the wondrous eternity that awaits.

Chapter Twelve

◆

Divine connection

"I am always in the right place at the right time to make divine connections with the right people."

Almost every day, I speak this declaration out loud to remind myself that I am following God's unique plan for me, and He is bringing it to pass. Though it's not an exact Scripture, it is a Biblical concept and a positive affirmation. It's abundantly clear at this point in my life, that those right connections have made all the difference in my walk with God, and in fulfilling His assignment for me.

There have been many preachers and teachers who have influenced my life at every stage. When I was a child, I had wonderful Bible teachers in Sunday School and Junior Church. I would not have been able to sing my testimony song, "I Came to Love You Early," had it not been for those godly women who told us Bible stories every Sunday. I will always be grateful for Miss Ruth, who had an amazing visual for every story she told. We called them flannel boards, or felt boards, and sadly, I don't think they are used much anymore. Miss Ruth's were wonderful. Many of the backgrounds she used contained hidden scenes that only showed up at the end of the story when she turned on the black-light attached to the top of the board. Talk about making the Bible come alive!

The one I remember the most was the story in II Kings 2 about the flaming chariot that bore Elijah to Heaven before he even died! It wasn't until the last minute that we were able to see the scene in all its black-light glory; the whirlwind that carried Elijah to the chariot pulled by a team of fiery horses! Miss Ruth flipped the switch and there they were! I still get goose bumps thinking about it!

There was also the story in Mark 9, of the disciples, Peter, James, and John, who went with Jesus one day to a high mountain. Gorgeous colors and swirls of God's Glory suddenly surrounded Jesus, Elijah, and Moses! The moment the black-light popped on over Miss Ruth's flannel board, we were mesmerized by the glowing scenes it created. It's probably one reason why I remember so many Bible stories today.

As a teen, I was greatly influenced by church youth leaders and especially Youth for Christ staff. Though I'd been a Christian since I was eight, I attribute my staying on the straight and narrow path through my teenage years to those men and women who invested their time and interest in the lives of young people.

After Dennis and I met and began dating in high school, we took turns attending the churches in which we each grew up. After we were married, we worked in music and youth services in a couple different denominations. By the time Stacie was two years old, most Sundays we were on the road singing with the Messengers, and weren't in our home church to be fed the Word of God. I still had a daily quiet time out of habit, but in the years of being a young mother, in a singing ministry, and working at the library, I didn't take the time I should have. I was still saved and going to Heaven, but I knew there was something missing in my relationship with God.

When Dennis was going through his brain surgeries in 1992 and 1998, we began to watch a few preachers and teachers on television on a daily basis. (Details of those surgeries are included in *I Will Not Fear: A Chosen Life.*) I learned quickly who resonated with my spirit and who did not. Billy Graham was one of the first preachers I heard on television and he probably led more people to the Lord than many TV preachers ever will. Television evangelism is needed for those who don't have a church home, are homebound, or for those who want added instruction from the Word of God. Sadly, a few have used media ministries for their own benefit, not because they answered a call to reach the world with the Gospel. We must be discerning and ask the Lord for divine connections with the right people and ministries, whether you listen to their messages on any media outlet or in person. I connected with the message of a few who taught things I hadn't been taught at church before. It was what I learned from those men and women that made me long to live in the Presence of God, be led by the Holy Spirit in every experience of life, and make the Word of God final authority in my life.

It amazes me when I hear the same message from more than one preacher, or I read the same thing in my Bible or another book or daily devotion. That's not a coincidence. Many times God orchestrates a divine connection between what He puts on his preachers' and teachers' hearts to share and when I access those teachings. We have a God of what, where, and when! Many times I have heard on the same day or week, from multiple sources the same exact message from His Word that I needed, and that God wanted me to hear—divine connections.

Hearing and hearing (Romans 10:17) is the way the Holy Spirit grows our faith and connects us to the right message and people. Many times God uses more than one source to bring across His Word to us and get it down deep in our hearts. Sometimes it takes many repetitions to get us to listen. Other times, we hear a message, it resonates immediately with our spirits, and we know that what that minister imparts into our lives will help us grow spiritually and complete our God-given assignments. Ideally our first and main connection is with our pastor and church, but God also uses others to speak to us.

One of those teachers who has been a divine connection for me is Rick Renner. He and his family live, minister, and teach in the former Soviet

Union. But he reaches the world through many media outlets. He is a Greek scholar and digs out the original meaning of words in the Bible. I found Pastor Rick's books through another ministry and since then, his books and teaching have helped me so much, both as a Christian and as a writer.

In his book, *The Will of God*, Pastor Rick talks about the way God uses past experiences and the places we've been to provide training ground and foundational skills to succeed in whatever God has called us to do. He says, "The surroundings and conditions in which you live and operate are important! Being in the right place at the right time... is critical for fulfilling His will. God will use specific people and places...to shape you, sharpen you, and prepare you to do His will."

In the same book, Pastor Rick reminds us that, "You will find that when you step out to obey what God has told you to do, He will supernaturally establish divine connections with other believers assigned to help you fully accomplish His will." Later in the book he writes, "We each are anointed to do our part."

In 1 Corinthians 3:6, the Apostle Paul said, "I planted, Apollos watered, but God gave the increase." They each had their part to do and those parts were connected, but they needed each other to complete the process. In one of Pastor Rick's daily devotionals, *Sparkling Gems from the Greek,* I read that, "It takes every one of us doing his or her different job—with God's blessing on it—for doors to open and harvests to be reaped. Divine connections are essential for completing a divine assignment."

At the end of every devotional in *Sparkling Gems*, Pastor Rick supplies a prayer. This prayer took a lot of pressure off of me in thinking that I had to do everything on my own to fulfill my purpose and assignment. God already had provided people out there to help.

"Father, I see that it takes divine connections to make a project of faith come to pass and bear fruit. I ask that You connect me to others who will respond to Your voice...to help me complete the assignment You have given me. I ask You to strengthen me and those with whom You will connect me, so that together we can do our respective parts under Your direction to fulfill what You want each of us to do."

As Paul said, it takes all of us to do our part, but it is God who gives the increase. I would not be where I am or doing what I am without divine connections to others.

When we began to seek where the Lord wanted us and what He wanted us to do, we heard a preacher say, "Find your church first. Everything you need to complete your assignment is connected to that church." We had no idea how true that would be.

After Stacie moved to Heaven, we prayed about and visited probably twenty churches for three years. In every place Dennis applied for a teaching job in a four-state area, we first visited nearby churches. A couple of the pastors and congregations were right for a short season. The teaching was sound and the music was all right, if not what we were familiar with and preferred. We were grateful they were there at the time. But we weren't at home.

We found our church through another ministry connection. Len and Cathy Mink had been at the same Christian radio rally where the Macs sang together for the very last time. We'd been asked months before, but it was only through sheer determination that Stacie insisted we go sing the National Anthem to open the service. It was one of our trademarks. Over Den's coaching years, we sang his acapella arrangement of the National Anthem at the beginning of many of his basketball games. (There are links on my website to my Facebook page and Youtube channel. Both have videos of our next to the last performance. It was at a basketball game and Stacie wore one of her signature hats.) I'm very patriotic anyway, but this is why it hurts me so much to see disrespect for the National Anthem and the flag. I love our country and always want to honor those who died for our freedom, but more than that, singing the National Anthem was a very special part of our ministry with Stacie.

Just a few days before she moved Home to Heaven, though she was very weak she wanted to sing it again. That was the day that we met the Minks and Gospel Duck, Len's adorable puppet. If

Stacie had felt better, we would have stayed, but we had to leave soon after we sang. The last thing we heard was Gospel Duck asking Len to pray for Stacie. She loved that.

Because of the divine connection on that very special day with our daughter, we decided to visit Cherokee Bible Church where Len and Cathy were scheduled to minister the Sunday before their annual Blue Ridge Parkway Motorcycle Ride. Because of the Holy Spirit atmosphere, the anointed teaching of the Word, the loving people, and especially the music, we knew the minute we arrived that we had found our church home.

As we searched for land and whatever God had for us here, our pastor's wife often told us, "You are always at the right place at the right time!" It's something she says to everyone as an example of a positive declaration we should all say and believe. Those words were exactly what we needed to confirm that we were on the right path. From the time we shared our vision with our pastor, he told us that we didn't have to do this assignment alone.

As Dennis and I pursue our new assignment, our "re-firement" assignment, there's not a doubt in either of our minds that we will need divine connections to complete it. Dennis wanted to be our general contractor, but he needs help building the ministry house. As I write this, there are three men out in the hot sun, putting up a concrete block crawl space. Know where we found those helpers? Cherokee Bible Church. Right now, along with two others from CBC, Pastor Randy is out in our yard, working to help us begin our construction project. He is a man of the Word, and a man of his word. (FYI, the character of General Rand in Book III of the *Tresia* series was inspired by Pastor Randy.)

Now that we have been at CBC for several years, we have seen the fruit of that connection. We expect many more connections to come. And it's a two-way street. Just as we support our church and other ministries, we expect our ministry at Macs MountainView to be a divine connection for the household of faith, our community, and anyone else God brings across our path.

It's an exciting adventure to be in the right place at the right time to make divine connections with the right people. Declare it every day. As Mark 11:24 says, *"...whatever things you ask when you pray, believe that you receive them, and you will have them."*

Chapter Thirteen

◆

Warrior Connection

If there is one type of music that can always bring tears to my eyes, it is a patriotic song. Whether they are Sousa's marches or songs about our country or our flag, each one holds a special place in my heart. I always get misty when music leaders or singing groups perform the anthems of the U.S. Armed Forces on special patriotic holidays. They ask members of the audience who have served in each branch of the military to stand when they hear their song. Most of the time, the veterans in attendance proudly stand and wave or nod at each other. All of them share a special bond, but you can tell there is a certain camaraderie between the men and women who were in the same branch of the military. It's a wonderful tribute to all those who have served our country. I never tire of watching this tribute to America's strong and brave soldiers of the past and present.

My dad was in the Air Force, so I grew up hearing, "Off we go into the wild blue yonder!" I remember the day he took us to see the Blue Angels at Forbes Air Force Base in Topeka. This select group of accomplished military pilots still performs amazing and daring feats with their fighter jets. On that day, to my little girl eyes, it looked like their wings touched as they flew in a close ornate formation. When they split apart in solo flight and soared through the crisp blue sky, the sound filled the air and the plume of smoke that trailed behind each jet made brilliant white criss-cross patterns. It was quite a thrill for a young girl. For my dad, too.

I still have my dad's Air Force uniform packed away in a bin somewhere. I wear his green fatigue hat sometimes. I'm proud to be the daughter of a veteran. Dad was stationed in Casablanca during the Korean War. He didn't see the battlefront, but he served proudly in the administration offices in Africa. I have many photos and memorabilia from the area that he kept from his time there. I wrote an article based on a couple letters my dad wrote while he was overseas. One letter was to my mother, his fiancée at the time.

The other letter he wrote was to a congressman in Washington D.C. My dad was an easy-going guy most of the time, but when it came to politics, he had some things to say! Apparently, his time in service was no exception. After I read their correspondence, I did a little more research about the base where Dad was stationed and their purpose in the war effort. His letters described the deplorable conditions that he was hoping to change by writing to the congressman. I was reminded how much Daddy liked to write. I guess I came by it naturally. There was a brief reply from the office in Washington, but the man in charge did not see his way clear to provide for any of the suggestions Dad made. Imagine that.

My dad has been in Heaven for over twenty-five years. I'm glad he does not have to be concerned about politics these days. I know without a shadow of doubt, he would not only stand for the Air Force Anthem, he would stand for the National Anthem and the Pledge of Allegiance. He believed in one nation under God and passed that staunch patriotism to me.

Did you ever sing the Sunday School song, "I'm in the Lord's Army?" It was a favorite of mine, and as kids we sang it with all the gusto and honor of any of the United States Armed Forces anthems. The words reminded us that even though we were young, if we had made the choice to make Jesus our Savior, we were soldiers in the Lord's Army! There was a line about marching in the infantry and riding in the cavalry, but my favorite was how, just like the Blue Angels, we could "ZOOM o'er the enemy!"

We also learned about the Armor of God. One of my teachers had an actual metal statue of an armored knight. He'd point out each part of the armor and teach us about the Helmet of Salvation, the Shield of Faith, and the Sword of the Spirit. We took home an illustrated chart of a Roman soldier dressed for battle. Names of the various pieces of the Armor of God were written next to the particular weapon or protective armor it represented. We discovered that we were not only soldiers in the Lord's Army, but we could be mighty warriors with weapons to fight against the devil and his evil forces!

As adults, we can become experts at using the Armor of God every day to defeat the attacks of the devil.

The titles of my *Tresia* books may cause you to wonder how in the world a hat, an umbrella, and a cane are connected to the Armor of God. Even if, as the full titles declare, they are also remarkable, extraordinary, and magnificent, they are still plain everyday objects. That is, until they are gifted to a child, taken on a journey, and transformed by the power of the Word.

In the course of the three books, those everyday objects become mighty weapons in the hands of the young warriors, able to protect and assist the characters as they fight the enemy. I spent hours deciding on names for those everyday objects that would correspond with their counterparts in the Armor of God. The remarkable hat becomes the Covering of Deliverance; the extraordinary umbrella turns into the Shelter of Reliance; and when activated by the spoken word, the magnificent cane is transformed into the Blade of Revelation. I had a wonderful time with the Holy Spirit in my Kingdom Corner as we transformed a hat, umbrella, and a cane into powerful weapons of protection for their bearers and destruction to the enemy.

As children of God we must put on the Armor of God every day to keep the enemy from stealing, killing, or destroying our lives. (John 10:10) It starts with the Helmet of Salvation. We are covered by the blood of Jesus when we believe and are delivered from sin. The Shield of Faith is essential to quench the fiery darts of the devil and his hordes. The Sword of the Spirit is the greatest weapon we have against the enemy. It's the Word of God. And the devil hates hearing it spoken with confidence and faith!

The Armor of God is found in Ephesians 6:10-18. Every single piece has a purpose. God has provided whatever we need if we will take the time to "suit up" in the mornings before we face the day. I heard a Bible teacher say that it's the same as putting on your clothes in the morning. You have to purposely choose to put on the Armor of God every day.

That's why Kingdom Corner time is so important. The time we spend in the Presence of God and in His Word and prayer, is how we learn to use the weapons He has provided for us.

I found a note in Stacie's Bible next to the passage in Ephesians. She wrote that if you have on the Armor of God, it covers you completely. Satan doesn't know who is inside. Put the Word of God in your mouth and let the devil have it between the eyes!

The connection to having victory in this life is established when Jesus and the Holy Spirit come to live inside us at salvation. That's why the devil has no idea who is speaking out of that Helmet of

Salvation. He can't see who is talking, and if we use the Words of Jesus, we sound just like Him! Satan is very familiar with Jesus using the Sword of the Spirit on him. In Matthew 4, in the wilderness, the devil tried to tempt Jesus three times to do his bidding. Each time, Jesus answered, "It is written," and proceeded to slash him with the Word of God. Finally, after three attempts to get to Jesus and stop him from his task on earth, the devil gave up. Nothing is more powerful than speaking the Word out loud.

We can do the same thing! It takes study, practice, and daily awareness that you have this protective barrier, weapons that no foe can withstand, and the authority to use them.

It's always best to go to the Word to learn about something first, but I suggest you get a copy of Rick Renner's book, *Dressed to Kill*. When I wrote my *Tresia* series, I used much of the information I gleaned from his knowledge of Roman weaponry and armor and how it applies to our spiritual armor.

It is sad that so many Christians live their lives in defeat when we have been given such a powerful protection against whatever the devil tries to do to us. How do we get connected to the power that is at our fingertips? Open our Bibles. Find out what God has provided in His Word. Dig out the verses that tell you what you have in Christ. Look up and read about righteousness, love, protection, provision, peace, joy, victory, and power. Then take those things for yourself and practice having and using them to accomplish your Kingdom assignment. Do you think Roman soldiers just grew up and knew how to fight on their own? Do the men and women who signed up to serve our country get rushed right into a war without any preparation?

Your Kingdom Corner is Boot Camp. It takes time every day for basic training. The Holy Spirit is our drill sergeant. God wants us to succeed and have victory, but He requires a willing heart to learn Kingdom ways and loyalty to His Name. With loving, caring, and compassionate determination, He will prepare, guide, and show you how to fight life's battles.

Soldiers don't have to bring their own uniforms, weapons, food, or shelter. Those things are provided. They signed up to serve their country and do whatever it takes to protect its citizens. Hopefully, those citizens are grateful for their service and show respect for the soldier. But even if they don't, it's the job they signed up for, and they will do it. Being a soldier is hard work and takes years out of a lifetime. Sometimes it even takes a life. But the job is an honor and privilege and comes with benefits.

If you are a child of God, you signed up to join the Lord's Army. It's time to train and receive our orders and assignments from our Commander and Creator. Time spent in His Presence is our connection to God's power, plan, provision, protection, and promotion. Get busy in your Kingdom Corner. Prepare for battle. It's time to become warriors and bring a lost world to our wonderful Lord before the final battle.

Chapter Fourteen

———————◆———————

Calling Connection

Every day in my Kingdom Corner, I read out loud a few verses from the Apostle Paul's prayers found in Ephesians 1:17-22 and 3:16-20. I looked up those passages in several translations and pulled out the phrases from each that especially spoke to my heart. Then I wrote out a personalized prayer based on those verses. I read a portion every day, Monday-Saturday, for myself and for others. This is my Monday prayer:

"I pray to you, God of Glory. Grant us a spirit of wisdom and revelation, insight into the mysteries and secrets in the deep and intimate knowledge of You. Flood our eyes with light so they are focused and clear, that we can see exactly what it is that You are calling us to do."

This is one of the ways that I use my Kingdom Corner time. I believe with all my heart that my time spent in God's Presence reveals the mysteries of knowing and walking with Him. Time with Him empowers me to live a life of faith without fear. Fellowship with Him and His Word opens my eyes, makes my steps sure, and lights my path so I can follow the plan He has for me. For almost six decades, I have made my time with God a priority. Some years I didn't do as well as I should, but in this season of my life, Kingdom Corner time is my anchor. Without my time spent alone with God every day, I would be lost. And I probably would not be doing what He's called me to do.

I've had many jobs over the years: receptionist, flower shop girl, waitress, pizza maker, legal secretary, teacher's aide, Avon rep, youth leader, singer, delivery person, managing editor, music teacher, library director, caregiver, and substitute teacher. Some of those were God things, especially the ones that I would normally have had to have a college degree to do, such as music teacher and library director. But God had a plan. He knew exactly what I needed and made a way for me to gain whatever knowledge and experience was necessary to fulfill my calling.

I am a writer.

Every job, every place, every life experience, every person I've ever met, has led me to this calling of writing books. I didn't realize it until pretty late in life. I didn't grow up saying "I want to be an author!" But from this vantage point of retirement, I see clearly the steps I took in my life were ordered by the Lord and led me here.

It's amazing to me that this is my sixth book. When I go back into my memories or tap my imagination, I hope to create a story that will further the Kingdom of God, strengthen spirits, satisfy souls, and entertain as it does so. Where do particular memories or creations from my imagination come from? They begin in my Kingdom Corner. Every book I have written was birthed in that secret place where the Holy Spirit becomes my co-author. I know this because I could never have come up with the concepts in my books on my own.

A God-given natural talent to write, or to do anything else, is certainly helpful. But if God has given you a dream, a longing to do or be something in particular, you must take time to develop your talent, learn your craft, practice using it, and pursue excellence in the process. This happens from the moment you feel called to begin until the moment you depart to Heaven! Never stop learning, improving, and reaching toward your goal and dream.

Kingdom Corner time is when I discover what God wants me to write. It is where He downloads the spiritual truths that He wants woven through my story. For me, there would never have been a first book had it not been for inspiration from the Word of God and prayer. *Dawn of Day* was inspired by the stories my mother told me about her childhood. It was her desire that I write a book about it. The Holy Spirit urged me to do the research and get it done. Mom was already in Heaven, but over the years, she had planted the seeds of the story. They were cultivated by time in my Kingdom Corner where I was able to grow them into a story about my mother and her sister and their heritage of living in an area in Kansas where the Underground Railroad was active. I had never wanted to write historical fiction, but I knew this was my first writing assignment.

Dawn of Day was released just a couple months before Stacie moved to Heaven. I didn't really have time or inclination to celebrate that milestone. My heart was already being prepared to write Stacie's testimony book. The themes and format for *I Will Not Fear: A Chosen Life* were also given to me in my Kingdom Corner. The fact that I was able to write and publish it less than a year after Stacie moved to Heaven, was evidence that God wanted it written. He has used Stacie's story to help so many people. I love hearing from readers who have read it and told me how much it changed their perspective on loved ones in Heaven. Stacie's story gave them hope.

The Macs, our family trio, sang a song titled, "The Glory Goes to You," written by Cyle Cornish. Stacie had picked it out for our second CD, and she and I sang the verses. The chorus states:

"I'm glad to be a part of every moment when Your love has touched a heart. But every single time, the pleasure has been mine, but the Glory goes to You."

As I wrote those words here, I had to pull out the CD and listen. Stacie's verse talks about how we may not know until we get to Heaven how many hearts were touched by seeds we planted. Through my tears I lifted my hands and praised the

Lord. Stacie already knows how many hearts were touched by her life and music! She probably knows every time another heart is touched and comes to Jesus when they read her book or listen to her voice sing songs about Jesus. I am so grateful we have those two CDs. God knew her voice needed to be heard until He comes.

Most of what we say and do will eventually be forgotten. But what we write down and, I will add, record for generations to come, those written or musical whispers from our hearts will last long after we are gone.

The *Tresia* series had been rolling around in my mind since I was in Junior High. One afternoon I drew a little cartoon character named Winny. She had a funny hat and held a sign that could convey whatever message I wanted to write on it. I added Winny to things such as notes in Stacie's lunchbox, advertising events at the library, and at the top of letters I wrote to Stacie in college and when she moved to North Carolina. Stacie loved Winny and her notes.

Around 2001, when the seeds of being a writer began to grow in my heart, I decided to write a book about Winny. Several friends had encouraged my writing after I left my library job, and some even mentioned that I should write my little character's story. Winny and her hat first became a picture book. Over the next ten years, and after many rejections from publishers, I realized that she needed more than a picture book. Winny's story developed into a three-book middle-grade inspirational fantasy series (for all ages.)

My first publications were historical fiction and a memoir. Both of these were genres I needed to write, but wasn't called to continue doing so. With inspirational fantasy I knew I had found my niche. I soon discovered that *Tresia* is my brand, as the business and especially the writing world calls what our writing is known for. I am called to write stories with spiritual truths woven into the backdrop of a mystical realm. The books by C.S. Lewis, Tolkien, Terry Brooks, and George MacDonald are my favorites. I may not ever come close to garnering a reader's love for Narnia, Middle Earth, Shannara, or Fairyland, but I know writing similar books is how God wants me to fulfill my Kingdom assignment.

When I began writing the *Tresia* books, I soon found out that names would be a critical element. Parents spend a lot of time choosing a name for a new baby. They usually decide on a name way ahead of delivery. Research is done into the meaning of names, and possible family names that might be passed down are considered. Or maybe it's just a favorite name from something in the couple's past, or a name they heard and liked. There are scores of books and online resources to find the perfect name for a child.

I use a baby name book in identifying my characters. Sometimes, I know the name I want to use, but for me, the meaning of the name is as important as the name itself. I also like to study out the

Hebrew meaning of names as well as the Greek meaning, as these two were languages of early Bible times.

The church I grew up in was a hymn and chorus singing church. We had Sunday Night Sings on a regular basis where congregants would call out a number in the hymnal and we would spend the entire service singing song after song. One favorite was a hymn called, "There's a New Name Written Down in Glory." I suppose the words to this song have rolled around in my head for decades. Perhaps that's why the term "new name" has stuck with me and ended up in my books.

In Revelation 2:17, the CEV says this: *"To everyone who wins the victory...I will also give a white stone with a new name written on it."*

Jesus promises in this verse to give to every person who overcomes in life, a white stone with a new name written on it. We don't know exactly what this verse means, but I checked several commentaries on the subject. Most agreed that it came from athletic contests in Roman times. It was a custom that the winners were given a white stone inscribed with their name. This stone served as a "ticket" to enter the rewards celebration later on.

The analogy that our new name is our ticket to the rewards ceremony in Heaven is something to be meditated on in a Kingdom Corner!

I didn't use the stone in my stories, but I wanted to include the new name concept. I pondered what this would be like for my characters.

In other books I've read, a special name is given to God by the character, or God gives special names to the characters. For me, new names portray a deeper dimension of relationship.

In my *Tresia* series, the children are given new names at the end of their journeys. I came up with these new names based on the actual meaning of their given names, as well as adding a spiritual aspect to the meaning. Many of my character names are borrowed from family and friends. The good characters only!

I have a photo of a cup that says, "I'm a writer. Anything you say or do could end up in a book." That's true. Most writers have bits and pieces of their lives scattered throughout their stories. But I hope that the names of family and friends that I have given to my characters, and especially their new names, made their inclusion in my stories more of an honor, rather than making good on a threat!

One of Stacie's dearest and oldest friends, Carol, is now my webmaster. She calls me Momma Mac. Her daughters call me Grandma Mac and both Caity and Ema were on my Youth Advisory Board for the *Tresia* books. I named characters after the three of them. Carol told me she was touched and became misty-eyed when she read the "new names" that the characters Caity and Ema were given in the "Kingdom Beyond Time."

That response is exactly what I hope to accomplish. As a writer, if I can touch a heart, then I've done my job. The lyrics to "The Glory Goes to You" apply here also.

It was in my Kingdom Corner that I discovered how important names are to God. Stories about Bible names and new names planted seeds for my writing while I read, prayed, and spent time with Him. This happens all the time.

In II Timothy, chapter one, Paul writes to the young preacher he called his son. They weren't related, but they were family. Paul tells Timothy to remember the genuine faith that was in his grandmother Lois and his mother Eunice, which was passed down to him. He reminds Timothy to stir up the gift of God which is in him.

The characters of Gran and Aunt Ardus were inspired by my paternal grandmother and aunt. These two characters are the Vanguards of the children in the stories. They go into their Kingdom Corners and pray, or speak Wind Words over their families. It is their Kingdom assignment.

Vanguards are soldiers who march in front of the army. Even though the *Tresia* books are written for middle-grades, the characters of Gran and Aunt Ardus have been embraced by many adults who are called to go before their kids, grandkids, nieces, and nephews, and adopted kids, to cover them in prayer as they march onto the battlefield of life.

I don't have any natural children or grandchildren here on earth. But God has blessed me with a niece and two nephews who are creating ongoing additions to the family! I also have many adopted kids, grandkids, and even great-grandkids—sixty-four at last count! These precious people are Stacie's friends and former students, as well as our dear friends and their families, who have adopted us and count us family. These are the names listed in my prayer journal. I lift them up to God in prayer every day. I am their Vanguard. I call them by name, going before them in battle.

I am called to be a writer, a Kingdom Keeper, and a Vanguard who wields Wind Words! I can only accomplish these three Kingdom assignments through time spent with God in my Kingdom Corner.

Dwelling in His Presence is my greatest calling.

Chapter Fifteen

◆

Kingdom Corner Connection

My dad loved to read. He also enjoyed working for the State of Kansas in the Data Processing Center. That was in the day when one computer filled an entire temperature-controlled room! Daddy just missed the era of personal PCs and laptops, though he got a glimpse of what was coming before he moved to Heaven in 1993. I remember when he "borrowed" one of the first laptops from the library. He was mesmerized. I believe he would have been an awesome librarian or bookshop owner. If he'd stayed here, maybe we would have opened a bookshop together. Daddy loved the written word and the written Word.

Dad sitting in his chair reading a book is one of my favorite memories of him. When I was little, I crawled into his lap and he read to me. When I visited my parents as an adult, Daddy was in his study doing one of three things: reading, listening to his police radios, or talking on his Ham radio. He started with a police scanner. Chasing police calls was a form of entertainment for our young family on a budget! In his later years, when he became a Ham radio operator, he enjoyed talking to other operators around the globe. I inherited his radio and, except for a few that my brother wanted, all of his books. Dad read mostly non-fiction, but there were several volumes of fiction from a 1950's book club, including quite a few westerns.

Recently, I inherited several books from Uncle Lindy, my dad's younger brother, a Zane Grey fan. My cousins agreed to give me his collection since I already had several of Grey's books that had belonged to my dad. I was amazed when I opened the box. I put Uncle Lindy's books with the ones my dad owned, and out of twenty books only three were duplicate titles! (I passed them on to my pastor who also enjoys old westerns.) I don't know if Uncle Lindy was influenced by Daddy or the other way around, but it made me smile to know that they liked the same author. I will continue to collect Zane Grey.

I'm a collector because I'm sentimental. I received my first Raggedy Ann when I was very young. I still have her. She is quite raggedy! All things Raggedy Ann and Andy became my first collection and Stacie's nursery décor. Later, I began collecting rocks from special places I've been. After inheriting a few ceramic angels, I started a collection, especially of angels holding books! My angels have been packed away for a decade, but I received an angel holding a book from an unexpected source who didn't even know I collected angels. It was from the sister of my high school friend, Kathy. Kathy and her husband Dave, who was Den's childhood buddy and best man at our wedding, also have a daughter in Heaven, born six months before Stacie. We've been friends since we were kids, but now we have a special bond with our girls waiting for us in Heaven. Kathy's sister felt like God wanted her to give me one of the angels she had bought at a close-out sale. Kathy asked if she had one with a book. She did. It was a God hug. That angel sits on my desk in my book barn. I couldn't pack it away.

From my days as a library director, I began a collection of Clifford the Big Red Dog and little statues of people and animals reading books. And of course, I collect books, especially by certain authors, as well as antique books.

I inherited Stacie's collections, too. She collected sandcastles, white roses, pigs, and Christmas holly dishes. I shared most of those collections with her friends. But, except for a few pieces I shared with her cousins, Stacie's Coca-Cola collection will be the décor for our guest house, Ruby Cottage.

My collections bring joy to my heart. I loved displaying them in my home and sharing them with guests. I've loaned my "Book people and animals collection" to a few libraries for their display cases. I will be glad when I have a place to display and share again.

A few years ago during my Kingdom Corner time, I asked the Lord what He collected. His answer was, "People's hearts and souls." It is my desire to add people and souls to my Lord's collection. I can do that by staying in the Lord's presence, tapping into his power, and walking out his plan for me by staying true to my calling. All of that takes place in my Kingdom Corner.

I recently read three books that were on sale in the general fiction section of a bookstore. I usually don't read books that don't have a spiritual aspect as part of the plot. Or at least I try to choose stories with a good moral view and something I can take from their pages that will help me grow as a person or believer. Thankfully, there are many books out there from amazing authors who feel the same way I do about the words we share. I want my stories to strengthen the spirit and satisfy the soul. (I used this as a tag line for several years before I changed it to reflect my *Tresia* brand.)

These three books, that I spent good money on, all had either "bookshop" or "library" in the title. I have a collection of books on these two subjects. (Imagine that…)

The first book was interesting, not something that stuck with me very long, but I remember a library and a nice plot. I kept it and put it on my shelf of "library" books. In the second was a bookshop, but I didn't get through three chapters before I'd had enough of the language and the situations the characters had put themselves in. I try not to fill my mind with things that give me a check in my spirit. I gave it away to another avid reader and included a disclaimer. The third was a great story about a library volunteer who helped people all the time, and wanted to work full-time in her library. Then the last few chapters revealed a couple secondary characters in a lifestyle I don't agree with. I know that people with opposing values are a fact of this world. As Kingdom citizens, it's our job to love people who may have different ways of thinking and living than we do. The characters in the book were very likeable, loving, and caring. But I'm not that audience or that writer. Just like the authors of those three books wrote from their worldview, and that's their choice, I must read and write from mine.

That's the thing about the Kingdom. We make our own choices about becoming citizens and obeying laws. Nobody is forced to do one thing or another, to believe a certain way or go down a different path. We all choose what to believe. We follow our own hearts, hopefully with the leading of the Holy Spirit. But the choice to believe in God and His plan is the only way we will receive any of the benefits of Kingdom living. And the Kingdom comes with benefits that are out of this world!

I wasn't forced to buy those three books just because I have a collection they fit into. The consequences for me were a bad conscience and money down the drain. A good lesson for me… sometimes a bookshop or library isn't the end all. From now on, I will do my best to only read and write from my heart. And what's in my heart is whatever is in the Word of God and is supported by the voice of the Holy Spirit.

I've had many different Kingdom Corners over the years. They have all connected me to my Father, through His Son and Holy Spirit. But I have a dream Kingdom Corner that I hope to create soon. It will be at the top of my log home in a loft, surrounded by bookshelves loaded with books, my collections, and photos of the people I love. It will contain my writing spot in one corner, with my desk and computer situated by a small window with a view of the mountains to gaze through and receive inspiration. A separate reading nook, nestled in the opposite corner by another window, is where I will curl up in a comfy rocking chair with my Bible, journal, and a cup of coffee. Perched on the corner of an antique table beside my chair will be the little lamp Stacie gave me with the reading rabbits. Large photo frames that hold my "literary" pictures of libraries and children reading will be spaced along the walls above the bookcases. A big vision board will be in the center of another wall, because once my dream Kingdom Corner is a reality, I will have a new vision to put on my board. Braided rugs will be tucked under everything in the entire loft, and the gable will hold the photographs and portraits of my ancestors. I have a collection of those, too.

I love "faithing" about my dream Kingdom Corner. The Vision *will* come to pass *soon*.

When I was in high school, I attended Youth for Christ camp in Woodland Park, Colorado. There was a trail there that I loved to walk. At the beginning was a sign. "Be Still and Know that I am God." That mountain trail was one of my first Kingdom Corners, and was one of the places where

I felt the tangible presence and power of God. As a teenager, I didn't know His plan for me yet, but I knew I wanted to follow it, whatever it was. I went back to that camp as an adult and walked that same trail. God's presence was still there.

That memory and a verse in Psalm 46:10, along with things the Holy Spirit has been talking to me about, has impressed on me that my "Word of the Year" for 2021 will be "Still." Being still and spending time in silence is not a natural thing for me. I need to learn how to find that quiet place deep inside my spirit, where I can hear the Holy Spirit's voice.

This year I'm reading a devotional commentary on the book of Mark by William Barclay. He called this concept of being still, "the rhythm of the Christian life." He added, "It is a continuous going into the Presence of God from the presence of men, then coming out to the presence of men from the Presence of God."

We spend time in the Presence of God to receive strength and wisdom to go out and serve Him in the presence of men. They support each other: stillness before God and service to mankind. Both are needed for a believer's life to flow.

I love the Message translation of Matthew 11:28-30.

"Are you tired? Worn out? Burned out on religion? Come to me. Get away with me and you'll recover your life. I'll show you how to take a real

rest. Walk with me and work with me…Learn the unforced rhythms of grace. I won't lay anything heavy or ill-fitting on you. Keep company with me and you'll learn to live freely and lightly."

That's the purpose of Kingdom Corner time.

It may not be in my dream Kingdom Corner yet, but wherever and whenever I meet with God, I want to cultivate the practice of being still. I believe it is one of the most important things any of us can do. To hear the voice of God as He speaks through His Word and through His Holy Spirit is vital to living a life that is pleasing to Him, one that He planned especially for us. John 10:10 concludes with these words: *"I have come that you may have life, and life more abundant."*

What a promise! I'm convinced that if we make it a priority in our lives to find that quiet place where we truly fellowship with God, it will lead us into new realms of wonder. Spend time in the Father's PRESENCE every day. Listen to the Master Storyteller speak as you read His Word and meditate on it. That's how to discover the POWER contained in His Word. He will be there with us, answer our questions, cleanse us, and change us. Talk to God in prayer through the Holy Spirit Who resides inside of you. Be still and know that He is God. Listen to what He has to say about the PLAN He has for your life. Then go out and do your God-given assignment.

Experience the Kingdom Corner Connection…
where wonder awaits.

PART III
The Connection

———◆———

Connect Points

Chapter Eleven: Beginnings Connection

Make a list of significant beginnings in your life. Can you see how God led you from one season of life to the beginning of a new one? In this chapter, I used the homes I've lived in over the years to mark the seasons. Can you pinpoint something that took you to new beginnings? (Relationships, jobs, health, moves, etc.) Journal or discuss your findings.

Did time spent with God help you in transitioning from one beginning to the next? If so, how did you see the hand of God moving in your life? Journal or share about something specific that the Holy Spirit spoke to you during quiet times with Him that led to a new beginning in your life.

In my Bible, I keep a list of "spiritual markers" that remind me of new beginnings or past victories. If you like that idea, make your own list and keep it in your Bible or journal. Refer back to it when you feel lost about what to do next. If God led you in the past, He will lead you to your next step.

Read Genesis 1 in several translations. If desired, read books about scientific and spiritual creation theories. Ask the Holy Spirit to help you see Creation from His perspective. Make notes as you study.

After reading, studying, and meditating on the different creation theories, this is the perspective that God gave me. After the fall of Lucifer and after however many years true science requires, the earth became without form and void. A brand new beginning formed in the mind and heart of God the Father-- a perfectly restored world. Jesus knows His Father's heart, and He spoke those creative thoughts into the empty atmosphere and filled it with His Words. Upon hearing the spoken Words of Jesus, the hovering Holy Spirit went to work and brought those thoughts and Words into being as recorded in the Genesis 1 account of Creation. I believe in the Gap or Restoration Theory where the Bible and science co-exist. It makes sense to me. Journal or discuss with friends your thoughts about God's Creation.

Chapter Twelve: Divine connection

Write out a declaration that you want to come to pass in your life, then say it every day. It can be based on Scripture or Biblical teaching or a motivational concept for success in life.

Remembering the people who have made an impact on you is a good way to practice a grateful life. List a few major divine connections with people in your life and how they have influenced you. Journal or share your thoughts. If those people are still here, take time to let them know what they have meant to you and why.

Is there a certain family member or friend, an author, speaker, or musician you have read or listened to who has been a great influence on your life? Think about or journal about things that you have learned from them. What can you do in return to say thank you for what they have done for you?

Can you think of a time when you were the one who planted a seed of kindness, love, or valuable information into someone's life, but there was little or no response? Such as, have you shared something or done a kind deed, but there was no response at the time? Did you think about how maybe you planted the first seed, God made it grow, and another saw the fruit? Journal about it, or come up with something you can do to plant a good seed in someone's life today.

Chapter Thirteen: Warrior Connection

Have you or someone you know well, served in the military? If it's you, thank you for your service. If it's someone you know, take time to thank them and maybe listen to a story or two about their active duty. Write about or record veterans' stories, then share them with a child. Talk about patriotism, honor and respect for the military, our country, and its flag.

Look up the words to the military anthems and read every stanza. Find the stories of when and why they were written. Listen to them online with a child and discuss the questions they may have.

Look up all the words to the Star-Spangled Banner and read the story behind it. Journal about what it means to you. Share with a child or a friend.

Look up Ephesians 6 and read about the Armor of God. List the pieces of armor and weapons. Journal what the Lord speaks to you about each one and how you can apply them to your life.

Create an activity to share with a child about the armor of God such as a chart or picture of a Roman soldier in battle dress. Discuss each piece of the armor and list practical things the Armor of God can do or how it can be used in a child's life.

Chapter Fourteen: Calling Connection

Read the prayers of Paul in Ephesians 1:16-22 and 3:16-20. Look them up in several translations. Personalize and write out a prayer based on those passages of Scripture that you can use to pray over yourself and others.

Think about the seasons of your life. What was your calling or assignment for each of those seasons? Journal or share with a friend what your dream or calling is.

If you aren't there yet, what steps can you take toward that dream or calling? If you are already experiencing it, how do you keep your calling fresh? How do you motivate yourself to keep your dream alive and well?

Look up the meaning of your name in a baby name book or online. Write the meaning down. Do you like your name? If you could choose a new name today, what would it be? Research the meaning of the name you would choose and write it down beside your given name and meaning. Does your life and personality reflect the meaning of either or both names? Journal your thoughts about your name or the one you would choose for yourself.

Revelation 2:17 is the promise that the victor, or overcomer, will receive a new name. What new name do you hope Jesus gives you? Journal or share with someone why you want that name and what Jesus would say to you about why He chose it for you.

Do you have a heritage of a faithful praying mama or grandma? Are you a praying parent or grandparent? If you want to be a Vanguard for children or adults in your life, create a Kingdom Corner or find a quiet place where you can meet with God and connect to the Kingdom on their behalf.

Chapter Fifteen: Kingdom Corner Connection

My dad was a great influence on my love of books and libraries. That influence became the foundation for my calling. Can you trace the foundation of your calling back to a certain person or experience? Journal or share.

If you are a collector, share your collections with a friend, or better yet, a child. Tell them how you started the collection and why you chose it.

I bought three books with "book or library" in the title just because I have collected those types of books in the past. I regretted it. Have you done something and/or spent money on a hobby or on a leisure activity or made an impulsive purchase that you later regretted? Think about or journal about why you made the decision to go ahead and do so, and why you regretted it later.

Because of my regrettable purchase of the three books, I decided to be more discretionary in my book buying in the future. Did you learn a lesson to help you make better decisions in the future? Journal about what you learned.

Is there a place you have been in the past that brought you special peace and you felt the presence of God? Journal about where it was and why it was special to you.

I have a dream Kingdom Corner in my heart and on my vision board. It's connected to the home we will build and the future books I will write. Think about your dream. If money was no object, and you could do or create anything you wanted, what would it be? Make a list. Writing down dreams and goals is the first step to making them happen.

I recommend making a vision board and keeping your dream in front of your eyes. If you don't want to do that right now, begin here: Find a photo of your dream house, trip, vacation, vehicle, or the book or song you want to write. Put it on your vision board or refrigerator and thank God for it every time you look at the photo. Or, create a place you can call your own and work on accomplishing your dream. A grateful heart is the second step to making your dream happen.

Whether or not you create a Kingdom Corner, I hope you will find a place and time where you regularly meet with God. Seek His presence, power, and plan for your life. God will meet you in that place and show you the mysteries and secrets of knowing Him. Journal or share with me or another friend the wonders and *Kingdom Corner Connections* you discover. I'd love to hear from you.

*"A light breeze began to blow through the room. A shaft of flickering flames encased in a soft blue glow rose from the rocking chair, through the ceiling and beyond. The **Connection** was established. She heard a still small Voice deep inside her spirit."*

Trinity Tales of Tresia,
Book II: A Quite Extraordinary Umbrella

Thanks from the Author

Thank you for reading *Kingdom Corner Connection*. After reading this book, I hope you have realized that God will meet you anywhere and anytime. If you put Him first and make your fellowship with Him a priority, He will use your time together to affect every part of your life. I pray that you have been inspired to create your own Kingdom Corner as a special meeting place where you connect every day with the Three in One.

I would love to hear from you. You can contact me on my website or by email. Keep up with me by signing up for my email newsletter and blog, plus links to my social media. You will find info about me and my books on my website, but there are also features created especially for you, so I hope you will take time to go and look around.

I am honored and humbled that God has given me six books (so far) to share with you. Writing is a solitary endeavor, but publishing is not. First, thank you from the bottom of my heart to those to whom this book is dedicated. What you have imparted into my life made much of the content possible to share. Thanks to my critique partners, Georgia Wilson and Maggie McKinney, and to my editor extraordinaire, Sheryl Riggs. You all make my writing shine. Thanks to my first and second (Alpha and Beta) readers, especially those who contributed reviews at the beginning of this book. I appreciate each of you for taking time to read, comment, and review the pre-pub edition. Thanks to Sherri Hutton at Rowe Publishing for sticking with me and creating the finished product. Thanks to Mark Iwig for the beautiful cover photo, and to Carol and Emalee Nelson for the perfect clip art compilation. Thanks to my family and friends and to my "Clan" of loyal readers and the readers I haven't yet met, for your prayers, support, and encouragement. Thanks to my Book Launch Clan for helping me get the word out about this book. And thank you in advance for posting online reviews! This helps an author more than you know.

Wherever you choose to do so, and whether you give that place a name or not, I hope you will connect to God's Presence for a while every day. Tap into His Power and seek His unique and amazing Plan for your life. In the days in which we live, those minutes or hours you spend with God will make all the difference in your perspective on life. Be BLESSED, my friend.

I would love to hear from you. You can contact me through the following:

www.jamcphail.com

www.facebook.com/jamcphailbooks

email: jamcphail@charter.net

About the Author

J.A. McPhail is a writer and published author. She is a graduate of the Rubart Writing Academy, a member of the Association of Christian Fiction Writers, and the North Carolina Storytelling Guild.

McPhail's first book was published in 2012. *Dawn of Day* is a middle-grade historical fiction novel about the Free State battle and the Underground Railroad in Kansas. Her second book, published at the end of 2013, is a memoir about her daughter, Stacie, titled, *I Will Not Fear: A Chosen Life*. *Trinity Tales of Tresia* trilogy is an upper middle-grade inspirational fantasy.

J.A. McPhail is a native of Kansas and a former public library director. She married her high school sweetheart, Dennis McPhail, a high school counselor, choral director, and coach. For over three decades they sang Southern Gospel music with the Messengers Quartet in Kansas, and later with their daughter Stacie as The Macs in North Carolina. Now the McPhail's write books and songs from their retirement home in the beautiful mountains of Western North Carolina.

Other Books by Author

Trinity Tales of Tresia Series

Book I – *A Most Remarkable Hat*
Book II – *A Quite Extraordinary Umbrella*
Book III – *A Perfectly Magnificent Cane*

Before the beginning of Time, they were Three in One. From the empty expanse of space They spoke into existence the Realms of Tresia; a home, but no family. So they created children and gave them gifts.

I Will Not Fear

She arrived late-over three weeks past her due date – and she departed decades too early for her family and friends. But during the 36 years of her life on earth, Stacie Jeanne McPhail brought love and joy to everyone who knew her.

I Will Not Fear: A Chosen Life is a testimony to the faithfulness of God. It is the fulfillment of a mother's promise to her only child, to share with others why and how this family chose, no matter what, to live a life of faith without fear.

Visit the author's website at
www.jamcphail.com for more information.

Dawn of Day

Henrietta never liked history. But on a late summer day in 1932, she and her sometimes annoying little sister Irma Jean, hear an exciting true story from their artist friend, Maude Mitchell—a story that takes them back in time 75 years.

In 1856, Maude's father, William Mitchell, came from Connecticut to support the Free State cause in Kansas. William and his sister Agnes hid runaway slaves in their cabin, including Jesse and Abby, two slave children who'd been cruelly separated from their mother.

Henrietta had learned about the Underground Railroad at school, but she never realized how dangerous it was for everyone involved. But what has slavery got to do with the family secret and Aunt Jo being mad at her parents?

As the pieces of the puzzle begin to come together, Henrietta discovers a surprise from the past that nobody dreamed was possible.

Visit the author's website at
www.jamcphail.com for more information.

CPSIA information can be obtained
at www.ICGtesting.com
Printed in the USA
LVHW031107311220
675393LV00005B/766

9 781644 460122